Hit the grou
running assemblies

50 ready-to-use acts of collective worship for primary schools

Denis O'Gorman

kevin
mayhew

First published in 2006 by
KEVIN MAYHEW LTD
Buxhall, Stowmarket, Suffolk, IP14 3BW
E-mail: info@kevinmayhewltd.com
www.kevinmayhew.com

9 8 7 6 5 4 3 2 1 0

ISBN 1 84417 689 4
Catalogue No. 1500947

Cover design by Sara-Jane Came
Edited and typeset by Graham Harris

Printed and bound in Great Britain

Contents

Introduction

Hit The Ground Running contains 50 exciting stories and assemblies on themes of kindness, respect, sharing, friendship and caring for other people, suitable for children of all faiths and none. Each assembly includes a Bible reading and a few words for those who wish to conclude their assemblies with a prayer.

A Better Life

Femi was a very happy boy. He went to the village school in Catawba with his friends, Gerda, Hadhi, Ghipe and Habbibe. After school they went fishing and swimming in the lake. At night they sang songs round the village fire. They didn't have much but they were happy.

One night Mr Odofin and his wife, Hakika, said they were leaving and taking Femi with them. They were going abroad to earn more money and make a better life. Everyone was sad, especially Femi's gran.

When they got to Einstoven Femi's dad did very well and soon got a job driving buses through the crowded city. They earned enough to rent two rooms on the top of a tower block. Femi did well at school and made many friends, though some teased him because the Odofins, as yet, couldn't afford to buy him super trainers, like the others had. He didn't dare tell them that in Catawba children didn't wear shoes at all!

Mrs Odofin was pleased with their new life, but she didn't like the weather. It was always cold and raining in Einstoven.

Mr and Mrs Odofin worked very hard and earned enough money to go back to Catawba for a holiday. All the village came to greet them. Femi went swimming and fishing with his friends, Gerda, Hadhi, Ghipe and Habbibe. Femi thought it was lovely not to have to wear shoes again.

After two weeks the holiday was over and there was a farewell party in the village. Everyone was sad when it was time for them to go.

'I don't want to go,' said Femi. 'I want to stay here with my friends and with Grandad and Grandma.'

'I don't want to go either,' said Mrs Odofin.

'Neither do I,' said Mr Odofin, laughing, as he tore up their return tickets. 'Money doesn't matter if you have friends.'

THE POINT

It is better to have friends than things.

READING

Don't trust in money, but in the love God shares with us. *Paraphrase of 1 Timothy 6:17*

PRAYER

Father God,

You love us and give us everything we need. Help us to be grateful for what we have and to be kind to those who are not as lucky as us. *Amen.*

A Present for Mother's Day

Every evening when Mr Leyton came back from work he loved to spend time in the garden. He would go there at weekends, too, when he wasn't working. He grew carrots, cabbages, potatoes and peas, but pride of place was the corner of the garden where he grew the marrow.

Not that Mr Leyton liked marrows, but in Marrowton, there was a competition every year. It was called *The Marrowton Garden Festival* and everybody displayed what they had grown in their gardens. There were many prizes. The most important prize – a silver cup – was awarded for the biggest and best marrow, and Mr Leyton had won it every year.

At weekends, Philip, Carla and Sandra helped him, but they weren't allowed to go near the marrow. That needed special care. Little Timmy didn't really help because he was only three, but he had a toy wheelbarrow which he just pushed around the garden, thinking he was helping.

On Mother's Day the family decided to make it special, so Dad organised a barbecue in the garden, and Philip, Carla and Sandra planned what presents they could give to Mum. Philip gave her flowers, Carla gave her chocolates, and Sandra gave her a basket of fruit. Of course, little Timmy couldn't give her anything because he was only three and didn't have any pocket money.

Mum was thrilled and thanked the children for their presents. 'They show you love me,' she said.

Halfway through the barbecue Timmy toddled up to them with his toy wheelbarrow and fell over. Everyone laughed. Timmy got up and carried on pushing his wheelbarrow up the garden. With a lovely smile of joy he put the wheelbarrow in front of his mum.

There inside was the precious marrow! Dad couldn't believe his eyes! 'My precious marrow!' he wailed. 'It would have won first prize! Just another three weeks and it would have been perfect. It was my pride and joy! Now I won't even be able to enter it!'

Timmy couldn't understand why Dad wasn't pleased!

Mum smiled, however. 'Thank you, Timmy,' she said. 'It's a lovely present.' Then she turned to Dad and said,' 'Timmy is our pride and joy!'

THE POINT
Love is more important than any possessions.

READING
My children, our love should not be just words and talk; it must be true love, which shows itself in action. *1 John 3:18*

PRAYER
Father God,
Thank you for giving us so many good things. Help us to grow in your love. *Amen.*

The First Flight

Uncle Ken lived by the sea and loved to watch the seagulls. So did Jane, Jeremy, Hugh and Alicia, when they went to stay with him at weekends.

'Look at that,' he said. 'Little seagulls, just hatched. Soon, they will be ready to fly.'

When they looked, there they were – high up in the nest on the cliff top. Mum Seagull flew down every day and gave them a fish until, at last, they were ready to leave the nest.

One by one the little seagulls fell out of the nest – down, down, down to the sea. They opened their wings just before they reached the water and landed safely, where Dad Seagull fed them small pieces of fish.

The youngest little seagull wouldn't leave the nest. She was too frightened and afraid to jump. 'It doesn't matter,' she thought. 'Mum will bring me a fish every day, if I stay in the nest.'

But Mum didn't bring her any food! Indeed, she did come with a fish, but ate it herself – right in front of the little seagull, who was now very, very hungry.

'That's not fair,' said Hugh.

'That's really mean,' said Jane.

'Wait!' said Uncle Ken. 'Let's see what happens next.'

Later that day Mum Seagull returned with another fish in her beak. She flew around the nest but would not give any fish to her little one. She came right up to the nest, but every time the little seagull tried to catch the fish Mum Seagull flew away.

'That's really mean,' said Jeremy, looking through Uncle Ben's binoculars.

'Let's wait and see what happens next,' said Uncle Ken.

They could hardly believe what happened next! Mum Seagull flew by the nest with another fish in her beak. The little seagull was very hungry and forgot about the danger below. She jumped out of the nest and tried to take the fish from her mother's beak – but missed!

Down, down, down, she fell – down from the cliff to the rocks and waters below.

Alicia was horrified. 'She's going to fall on the rocks,' she cried.

'No. Let's watch and see,' said Uncle Ken.

Sure enough, just as the little seagull was about to crash, to her surprise, she opened her wings and landed safely.

There, she joined her brothers and sisters in the sea, where her proud dad fed her with little bits of fish – and Mum Seagull flew over them all with what seemed like cries of joy.

THE POINT

We are afraid of many things that we do not understand, but we can trust those who love us.

READING

Look at the birds: they do not sow seeds, gather a harvest and put it in barns; yet your Father in heaven takes care of them! *Matthew 6:26*

PRAYER

Father God,

We are often frightened. Help us to know that we are always safe in your hands. *Amen.*

Grandad's Duck

Jenny, Peter, Anne and Phillip were very excited. They were going to spend Christmas with Gran and Grandad. Grandad always did the cooking and was very good because he was once head chef at the Grand Hotel – but he liked everyone else to help.

When they arrived Grandad said: 'This year, I am going to cook you something special, but I want you all to help. We are going to have duck!'

Christmas Eve arrived and all the children helped Mum and Dad. They peeled the potatoes, carrots and onions, washed the sprouts and helped Grandad chop the oranges ready for the special sauce.

'The duck will be delivered first thing tomorrow morning,' Grandad said. 'It will be the most delicious Christmas dinner we've ever had!'

Sure enough, early next morning, a man arrived with a large cardboard box. 'One duck,' he said. 'Just as you ordered – delicious!'

When the man left they opened the box and out jumped the most beautiful duck you've ever seen! 'Quack! Quack! Quack!' it squawked as it ran around the room, as if delighted, at last, to find a family that would love and care for him. Grandad said: 'Well, we can't eat him, let's keep him and give him a name.' They all agreed to call him Henry and they took it in turns to stroke him.

So that year Christmas dinner was just vegetables and a home-made soup which Gran made quickly. They didn't mind. They had a new friend to love and care for and Grandad had a pet that followed him everywhere. After that, every year they looked forward to celebrating Christmas with Henry.

THE POINT

Love and friendship sometimes makes us have to give up other things we want. But to share love and friendship is better than anything else.

READING

Meanwhile these three remain: faith, hope, and love; and the greatest of these is love. *1 Corinthians 13:13.*

PRAYER

Father God,

We are your children. We believe in you. We trust in you. We love you. Make all the world one happy family, loving you and caring for one another. *Amen.*

Greedy Mr McCready

Two or three times a week Monica, Wayne, Janet and Ben went into Dobson's Village Store to buy a cake or a bar of chocolate before they caught the bus for school.

More often than not they would meet Mr McCready buying food for the day. He had cooked meat, cheese, bread and fruit all piled up on the counter. Then they'd see him fasten it all onto his bicycle before pedalling off onto the moors – obviously for his daily picnic. He never offered to buy anything for anyone else. No wonder they called him Greedy McCready.

'How could anyone eat all that food in one day and still stay slim?' said Mr Collard.

'It's probably because he spends so much time on his bicycle,' Mrs Wentworth replied.

'More likely because he gets sick every day, after eating so much!' said Mrs Gossiper.

Sometimes as the bus travelled over the moors it would pass him by, and everyone would shout, 'Greedy McCready!' through the windows.

Then one day they passed him by again, but this time it was different. He had fallen off his bicycle and was lying in the mud – and it looked as though he was hurt. There was food all over the road.

The bus driver had to stop. 'I'm sorry,' he said. 'I know you'll be late for school but we must get Greedy McCready to a safe place, call an ambulance and get all this food off the road.'

A bit further along, up a turning off the road, there was a little hamlet with a few houses, so the driver went there to get help. The children looked out of the window as the driver knocked on one of the doors.

A little old lady answered. 'We've got a man here,' said the driver, 'who's fallen off his bicycle. We need to call an ambulance.'

They helped him into the house and the lady said: 'Oh, poor Mr McCready! I wondered why you were late.'

By now, all the other neighbours had come into the house to see what was happening. Some were elderly, some were frail. 'Poor Mr McCready,' they kept saying.

The driver was puzzled. 'How come you all seem to know him?' he asked.

'Because he does our shopping every day,' they said.

THE POINT

Don't say bad things about other people. They might be nicer than you!

READING:

Do not judge others, so that God will not judge you, for God will judge you in the same way as you judge others, and he will apply to you the same rules you apply to others. *Matthew: 7:1*

PRAYER

God our Father,

You know each one of us and you love us. Help us to be kind and loving to everyone. *Amen.*

Hamid's Dream

Hamid was a very clever boy and most people liked him, but Kenny Marsh and Cindy Mellows didn't. They bullied him on the way home from school. Perhaps they were just jealous of him because he worked so hard and did so well at maths and English. Whatever the reason, they made his life a misery.

Like the other children from Mountview School, Hamid had to take the long way home, avoiding the Pineal Estate, where the children there would have set upon him if he had dared to try to go through the estate. Hamid couldn't understand why they couldn't all be friends.

Hamid was kind as well. On the way home every evening he stopped at Francesca's house. Francesca came from another country too, but not the same as his own. She was never very well and had to be helped around in a wheelchair. Often, she couldn't get to school, so Hamid would tell her what had happened that day and even help her with homework.

Hamid wanted to be friends and play with Francesca, but Francesca's dad said: 'No. Their religion isn't the same as ours.'

One night Hamid had a dream. He found himself in a lovely garden with beautiful flowers and fruit trees of every kind. It was full of children from every race, colour and country. He was amazed! He saw Kenny and Cindy splashing in the pool with the children from Pineal, and he jumped in to join them. He saw Francesca dancing on the lawn.

Then he woke up. He told his mum about his dream.

'Yes,' she said. 'That is how God wanted everything to be when he made the world and that is how it will be, when we are all together again.'

THE POINT

God created everything and it was good. Human beings have spoilt it – but the promise is that this is how eternal life will be.

READING

Then the one who sits on the throne said, 'And now I make all things new!'
Revelation 21:5

PRAYER

Father God,
You want all to be friends, but sometimes that is difficult. Help me to be kind and caring to everyone. *Amen.*

Hands up for God

On Thursdays Miss Naylor took Class 7 for RE, but she was off for two weeks so Mr Burton was going to have to take them instead. This was odd because Mr Burton had never taken RE before. He was the sports teacher and was not too sure how to do RE lessons.

The children were excited, because Mr Burton was their hero. Before he became a teacher he had been an Olympic boxer and had played rugby for his country. The papers used to call him *Bruiser Burton* because he was so tough in the ring and on the pitch.

Thursday arrived and Mr Burton came into the classroom. 'Well now,' he said. 'Let's start with a question. Hands up all the children in this class who believe in God.' No one put up their hand.

'OK, then let's talk about courage and fair play,' he said. That was much more his scene.

'Do you believe in God?' asked Aaarif.

'Now that's something I'd rather not discuss,' said Mr Burton.

On Friday evening Aaarif went with his dad to evening prayers in the mosque. He felt terrible and said this prayer to God: 'I'm sorry, Father God. I do believe in you, but I couldn't hold up my hand in class. No one else did. I was afraid everyone would stare at me.'

On Saturday David was in the synagogue and said: 'I'm sorry, Father God. I do believe in you but I couldn't hold up my hand in class. No one else did and I was afraid everyone would stare at me.'

On Sunday Catherine was in church. Silently, she said this prayer: 'I'm sorry, Father God. I do believe in you but I couldn't hold up my hand in class. No one else did and I was afraid everyone would stare at me.'

Just round the corner, Maria said the same prayer in another church.

The next Thursday Mr Burton said: 'Let's talk about courage and fair play.' He told them about his time as a boxer and rugby player and how you needed dedication and courage.

Then Aaarif put up his hand. 'Sir,' he said, 'last week you asked us to put up our hands if we believed in God. I didn't put my hand up, but I do!'

'So do I,' said David.

'Me too!' said Catherine, and Maria said the same.

'Now that's what I call courage,' said Mr Burton. 'Each one of you believes in God in different ways. He is your Father and so you are brothers and sisters.'

'But do you believe in God?' Aaarif asked again.

'Of course I do,' said Mr Burton.
'Then why didn't you tell us before?' said Catherine.
'Because I wanted you to say so first!' he said.

THE POINT

When we think that others will laugh at us, it is difficult to be brave and stand up for what we believe.

READING

I have told you this so that you will have peace by being united to me. The world will make you suffer. But be brave! I have defeated the world! *John 16:33*

PRAYER

Father God,
It is so difficult to be brave when others laugh at us. Please help us to be strong. *Amen.*

Happy Christmas

Most people in Sunnyvale thought that Ernie Smith was, to say the least, a little bit odd. You couldn't blame them, because Ernie used to celebrate Christmas every day of the year!

Even in the summer he would light up his Christmas tree and always have Christmas pudding for lunch. His house was full of Christmas cards and whenever he went out he would wish people 'Happy Christmas!' Even so, people didn't mind.

'Let him be,' they said. 'He doesn't understand that it's not Christmas.'

One day in August, Mum, Dad, Janet, Chris, Charlotte and Larry went to see him, as he lived near the seaside. 'When you come back from the beach, I'll have a lovely dinner ready for you all,' he said.

It was very hot and when the family got back Uncle Ernie had a lovely meal prepared – turkey, mince pies and Christmas pudding. He had lit a Christmas candle and had laid out Christmas crackers by each plate.

When they pulled the crackers and put on their paper hats, Uncle Ernie said: 'Happy Christmas!'

'But Uncle Ernie, it's not Christmas,' said Janet.

'Shhh!' Dad whispered. 'Be nice. He doesn't understand.'

They went to see him again on Easter Sunday. This time they thought he'd give them current cakes and Easter eggs. Instead he had prepared a lovely Christmas dinner, with all the trimmings.

'Happy Christmas!' said Uncle Ernie as he switched on the lights of the Christmas tree. This time, Dad had to say something.

'Uncle Ernie,' he said. 'You don't understand. It's not Christmas Day today – it's Easter Sunday!'

'I know!' Uncle Ernie replied. 'But if Jesus had not been born, he would not have lived among us. If he had not lived among us, he would not have died and come back to life again and then gone up to open the gates of heaven for us. That is why I celebrate Christmas every day.'

They all said: 'Happy Christmas, Uncle Ernie!'

THE POINT

Uncle Ernie knew the real meaning of Christmas – that Jesus came to die on the cross and save us all.

READING

At that time Jesus said, 'Father, Lord of heaven and earth! I thank you because you have shown to the unlearned what you have hidden from the wise and learned.' *Matthew 11:25*

PRAYER

Father God,

Thank you for sending Jesus into the world. Help us to live our lives the way he told us to. *Amen.*

His Lordship's Lady

Felicity Antonia Maples was highly respected in the village but nobody really liked her. She was always showing off. Every Saturday she came for tea in the village hall, though some were puzzled because she always came from Lord Baltimore's manor by bus.

Surely, they thought, she could come in a limousine and be driven by her personal chauffeur. But then, these high-up people often did odd things – just for fun, you know.

Even so, Kit, Jim, Jan and Terry liked to sit at her table and hear her stories about the past.

'Oh, yes,' she told them, 'I lived abroad in a beautiful mansion. I had lots of horses and went riding every day. I had servants and butlers at my beck and call and maids who brought my supper. I just had to click my fingers and I got anything I wanted. Now I live in Blantyre Manor and run Lord Baltimore's estate. I have a luxury apartment on the west wing so I still have servants and maids at my beck and call. They call me His Lordship's Lady.'

Then one Saturday, when Lady Maples came for tea at the hall, Kit noticed the lovely dress she was wearing. 'That's a nice dress,' she said.

'Oh, yes,' she replied. 'It cost me quite a lot of money.'

'But, Mum,' said Jim, 'that's the dress you gave to the charity shop! I can see the mark at the top where you mended it.'

Lady Maples' face went red and she ran out of the hall.

'Look what you've done!' said Mum. 'You've upset her. She probably gave a lot of money to the charity shop for that dress. High-up people do things like that. On Monday we'll take her some flowers to say we are sorry.'

So on Monday they went to Blantyre Manor. At the manor they rang the bell and a very snooty butler opened the door.

'Good morning. We've come with flowers for his Lordship's Lady,' said Mum.

'His Lordship doesn't have a lady,' said the butler. 'He lives here alone.'

'But we want to give these flowers to Lady Maples,' said Terry.

'Oh Maples!' said the butler. 'She's not here. She only comes in on Tuesdays and Fridays to do the washing. She used to help the other servants with cleaning the kitchens, but she is too old for that now.'

'Well, can you leave these flowers in her apartments?' said Jan.

'Maples does not have apartments here,' said the snooty butler. 'She lives just out of the estate – third hut on the right with a green door. You can take them there if you want to.'

The family made their way down the drive and found the huts. They noticed that the huts were old and needed another coat of paint on them. They knocked at the green door and Lady Maples opened it.

When she let them in they could tell she was ashamed of the tatty carpet and worn-out armchair in the corner.

'I am so sorry,' she said, as they looked around.

'Please, don't be sorry,' said Jan, as she put her arms round her. 'We've brought you these flowers. We love you much more, now we know you as you are, and not the horrible lady you pretended to be.'

THE POINT

Whoever, or whatever we are, we are precious in God's eyes.

THE READING

Aren't five sparrows sold for two pennies? Yet not one sparrow is forgotten by God. *Luke: 12:6*

PRAYER

Father God,
Thank you for loving us and making us special. *Amen.*

It's Not My Fault

On Thursday evening Angela took her children – Pauline, Tim, Rose and Tony – and their dog, Boca, to the swimming pool. There was a special place just outside, where people could leave their dogs on a lead.

Mum and the children had a wonderful time swimming and playing in the pool and time went by quickly.

Meanwhile Dad came home from work. He was tired and so he was glad to have a little time, all for himself. He thought he'd have a nice, warm bath before they all came home.

He went upstairs and started running the taps. Then the telephone rang and he came down to answer it.

'It's Angela,' Mum said. 'We're late and we've missed the last bus. Can you come and pick us up?'

'Oh, all right,' said Jack, but he wasn't very pleased. He drove out to pick them up, but Boca had slipped his lead and was running all over the place. It took them ages to catch him.

When they got home they opened the door and there was water everywhere – down the stairs and on to the carpet below. It took them half an hour to clear up the mess.

'If you hadn't been late and called me out to pick you up,' said Dad, 'this wouldn't have happened.'

'It's not my fault,' said Mum. 'I was ready but I had to wait for the children. They took so long getting changed.'

'It wasn't our fault!' said the girls. 'We were ready but we had to wait for the boys.'

'It wasn't my fault!' said Tony. 'Tim lost his sock and it took us ages to find it.'

'And it wasn't my fault!' said Tim. 'Boca slipped his lead and came into the locker room and took my sock and ran away.'

Ah-ha! That was the answer. It was all Boca's fault!

'You naughty, naughty dog!' they said. 'But for you this would never have happened!'

Of course, Boca didn't understand what they were saying but he knew they were cross with him and he must have done something wrong. He just crouched on the carpet and looked up at them with a mournful eye.

Then Mum picked up Boca and stroked him. She began to laugh. 'We can't blame Boca,' she said. Then, still laughing, she looked across the room at Dad and said: 'Come on, Jack! Own up. It was all your fault. You left the tap on.'

THE POINT:

When things go wrong, we often make excuses and try to find others to blame. We all make mistakes.

READING

I pray that your love will keep on growing more and more … *Philippians 1:9*

PRAYER

Father God,

You love us and help us when we make mistakes. Help us to love and forgive others when they make mistakes. *Amen.*

Meeting Mr Shuffle

The Wilkins family had booked their holiday to Campanula with Supertours. That included the return journey by coach, six days at the Mariana Hotel and a day trip to Faille for the Faille Festival.

In Faille Cathedral there was a gold statue of Jesus where you could lay down your prayer cards. There were colourful processions, with children in local costumes, and bands playing in the streets. In the evening there was a wonderful firework display. They were all looking forward to the trip. Cindy made a card to place before the statue, and so did Frank and Hannah. They wrote down things like – 'You are wonderful.' 'You are great.' 'Bless our family.'

Little James made one as well but he didn't really understand. He thought they were really going to see Jesus.

'No,' said Mum. 'It's only a statue. Jesus is in heaven – not down here.'

But James would have none of it. 'I'm going to see Jesus,' he told his friends at school and he wrote his own card. 'I like you,' it said.

While they were getting ready for their holiday they sometimes looked out of the window and saw Mr Shuffle going to the shop. That wasn't his real name because nobody knew his real name. He just 'shuffled' to the shop two or three times a week. That's why people called him Mr Shuffle.

Then the day before the Wilkins were supposed to leave they had a terrible shock. Supertours had closed down. They had lost everything. 'Sorry,' they said, 'there will be no holidays for anyone.'

The Wilkins were all in tears because they couldn't go on holiday. James was really upset because he still believed that they were going to see Jesus.

To make matters worse Sandra came round and told them she'd noticed Mr Shuffle hadn't been seen for three days. Dad went across the road to have a look. It wasn't hard. There was no lock on his door. Mum came too.

They saw Mr Shuffle all on his own, eating a little cream cake. 'I'm all right,' he said. 'It's my birthday today. I bought this cake as a special treat.'

'Why didn't you invite us to join you?' said Mum, looking around at the bleak room.

'Because I'm poor and lonely,' he said. 'Nobody would want to come and see me. There isn't even anybody to send me a card on my birthday.'

'Go and call the children,' Mum said. 'And bring over some cakes and the cards they made.'

'Thank you so much,' said Mr Shuffle, eating the cakes and looking at the cards.

That night Mum said to Dad: 'I'm glad we didn't go on holiday after all.'

'I'm not,' said little James, 'I wanted to go and see Jesus.'

'But you did!' said Dad.

THE POINT

Every time we help somebody we are doing God's will.

READING

The King will reply, 'I tell you, whenever you did this for one of the least important of these members of my family, you did it for me!' *Matthew 25:40*

PRAYER

Father God,
Please help me to be kind and loving to everybody. *Amen.*

Miss Dobson's Disgrace

All the parents in Newtown wanted to send their children to Blackmoor Primary School, especially as Miss Dobson and her staff got the best exam results in the town.

Miss Dobson insisted on hard work, fair play and respect for others, so when Andy Simpson came to school there was bound to be trouble. He was always up to mischief and didn't like the other children. Neither did they like him! They loved to see him get into trouble – which he often did.

Things went from bad to worse at the Monday morning assembly when Miss Dobson was talking to the children about care and respect. Nick and Pam gave Andy a push and sent him sprawling over the floor.

'Leave me alone!' he shouted. 'Why does everyone pick on me!'

'Andy Simpson! Come out here,' said Miss Dobson, and she told him off in front of all the staff and pupils.

Nick and Pam couldn't help smiling. 'Serves him right,' they thought.

At the tea break in the staffroom Mr Harris told Miss Dobson that it wasn't Andy's fault. 'He was pushed. I saw it happen. Perhaps, Miss Dobson, you should take him aside after school and apologise.'

'No, I won't!' she replied. 'But I will do so tomorrow.'

Next day in assembly Miss Dobson called out Andy Simpson and made him stand in front of the whole school. Nick and Pam smiled again.

'Andy Simpson,' she said. 'Yesterday I called you out in assembly for something that wasn't your fault. Now, in front of the whole school, I want to apologise and say I'm sorry.'

That happened many years ago and the names have been changed, but the story is true.

THE POINT:

It takes a lot of courage to say you were wrong.

READING:

If we say that we have not sinned, we make God out to be a liar, and his word is not in us. *1 John 1:10*

PRAYER

Father God,

You know we all do things that hurt other people. Help us to forgive and forget the hurts and be kind to everybody. *Amen.*

Mr Piccolo

When Karen, Joe, Beth and Ronny went on holiday to Magalia it seemed like a dream. The hotel they stayed in wasn't the best, but it was clean, tidy and all they could afford. It had a swimming pool and wasn't far from the beach.

Every day they bought fruit and cheese from the market for a picnic on the beach and in the evening they went to Alfredo's, where you get a pizza and ice cream for less than two euros. From there they could see the rich and famous ordering their evening meals and wine at the Alfresco Ristorante Imperiale on the other side of the square.

Every evening a little man (he said his name was Piccolo) came begging round the tables at Alfredo's and most people put a few coins in his hat. Dad said: 'I know we haven't got much, but we are better off than this poor man. We must care for the poor, so let's just have a pizza tonight, but no ice cream and give the money to Piccolo.'

And so they did, even though Ronny and Beth didn't really want to.

On the last night they went back to Alfredo's but Piccolo did not appear. The children were really glad. It meant they could have ice cream instead of giving their money to the beggar.

Then Ronny looked across the square at the Ristorante Imperiale. There was Mr Piccolo in a smart suit ordering dinner for himself and his friends.

'Look!' said Ronny. 'We've been fooled. Piccolo wasn't poor after all!'

'We gave up our ice creams because we thought he was poor,' said Karen.

'We wasted all our money,' said Beth, who was very angry.

'No, we didn't,' Dad said. 'We did what we thought was right. How were we to know?'

'But now we do know,' said Beth, who was still very cross. 'He isn't poor at all!'

'But he might have been,' said Dad.

THE POINT

Whatever we try to do for others with love and kindness, will never be forgotten by God our Father.

READING

We may seem to be fools to other people – but wise in trying to be like Jesus. *Paraphrase of 1 Corinthians 1:27*

PRAYER

Father God,
Help us to be kind to everyone, even when it's hard to be so. *Amen.*

Pastor Michael's Miracle

There weren't many people at Pastor Michael's church on Sunday morning but he preached his sermon just the same. On the way home, he met the mayor and they strolled through the park together.

'Why don't you come to church, Mr Mayor?' Pastor Michael asked. 'It would be a good example to the people of Littleton.

'I'd like to,' said the mayor, 'but that wouldn't be honest. You see, I don't believe in anything and I don't believe in miracles. If I could see one for myself, then perhaps I would come.'

'Right then,' said Pastor Michael. 'On Sunday the fourth of May, at six o'clock, in my garden next to the church, I will show you a miracle that you can see for yourself.'

'All right then,' said the mayor, 'I'll be there just to see.'

'It won't be that easy,' said Pastor Michael. 'I'll need your help before I show you the miracle. I'll need a huge granite rock hewn out of the quarry and placed in the middle of my lawn.'

'Oh, I can arrange that,' said the mayor – and he did.

Sandra, Darren, Kate and Terry watched their dads haul the heavy rock up the hill to Littleton. Others came out to help. Some thought it was just a load of nonsense and just laughed at the people struggling up the hill.

'I don't know,' said Sandra's dad as they put the heavy rock on the lawn. 'I have my doubts, but miracles do happen.'

All week the buzz went round town. On their way to work, people stopped and stared at the rock. Would they see a miracle or not? No one could agree.

As you can imagine, on the fourth of May nearly everyone was there in the garden. Crowds of them! The clock began to strike, one, two, three, four, five then six! Everyone stared at the rock. Nothing happened!

Some were disappointed! Some were angry! Some just laughed and said: 'I told you so!'

Then Pastor Michael came out of the house, carrying his little baby. 'Look!' he shouted. 'This is Amy, my little daughter. She was born three weeks ago! Isn't she beautiful? See her bright blue eyes and tiny feet and hands! Isn't she a miracle!'

Everybody clapped and celebrated. 'Yes, she is!' they shouted. Even the mayor himself joined in.

'I promised I'd show you a miracle today,' said Pastor Michael.

'Yes,' said the mayor, 'but I'm still puzzled. Why did you want the rock? What has that got to do with it?'

'It was to get you all together, and to celebrate a miracle!' said Pastor Michael.

THE POINT

We like to see things that are unusual, but sometimes we are so busy looking that we miss the miracles that are around us all the time.

READING

When I see the heavens and all the wonderful things you have made then I praise you with all my heart. Paraphrase of *Psalm 8*

PRAYER

Father God,

We are your children. We believe in you. Open our eyes to see the wonderful things you have created in our world. *Amen.*

Strangers in the Night

For Reverend Maynard the best part of Christmas was the children's service. The children brought up the cards they had made and placed them round the altar. Wendy had drawn a picture of the poor shepherds, who were the only ones to welcome Jesus.

Ken had drawn a picture of Mary, Joseph, and Jesus lying in a manger. Lucy had drawn a picture of Bethlehem covered in snow. Harry had drawn a picture of a grumpy man!

'Who's that?' said Reverend Maynard, and everybody laughed as he showed the picture to the people in church.

'That's the innkeeper,' said Harry, 'who wouldn't give Mary and Joseph a room for the night.'

'You're right,' said Reverend Maynard. 'Now you understand. Jesus came into the world and only poor shepherds welcomed him.'

Reverend Maynard had other services that day and to be honest he was quite glad when the last one was over. He put his feet up and watched TV until eleven o'clock. By then he was very tired and went to the kitchen to make himself a chocolate drink, before he went to bed for a good night's sleep.

Then the doorbell rang. 'Who on earth is this?' he said to himself, 'Coming here at this time of night – especially at Christmas!' He was quite angry.

Even so, he opened the door. 'What do you want?' he said rather sharply to the scruffy young man and young lady standing there.

'We're lost here in Kenbridge,' the young man said. 'We have no money and nowhere to go.'

'My little baby's hungry,' said the lady, 'and we have no milk.'

It was cold and beginning to snow, so Reverend Maynard thought he'd better let them in. The baby started to cry.

'This is not what I need,' he muttered to himself. But he couldn't really turn them out into the night. 'All right,' he said, 'you can sleep down here on the floor and there's some milk in the fridge. But you'd better be off in the morning. This is a church house – not a guest house. I'm off to bed.'

But that night he couldn't sleep. He heard the baby crying downstairs and the young couple moving around. Finally he got to sleep and slept like a log – until ten in the morning!

The couple had left. 'Thank God they've gone!' he thought. 'Now I'll have some coffee.' But when he opened the fridge there was no milk.

They'd used it all. That really did annoy him, but at least they'd gone. He really hoped they wouldn't come back again.

He made some toast and sat in the kitchen. Then he saw a note on the table. It said: 'Thank you for giving us a room last night. You were very kind. Sorry about the milk but baby was very hungry. We hope we didn't spoil your Christmas. Love from Joseph and Mary.'

POINT

Whatever we do for other people, we do for God.

READING

Whenever you did this for one of the least important of these members of my family, you did it for me! *Matthew 25:40*

PRAYER

Father God,

You love all people. Help us to love and care for those who are in need. *Amen.*

The Anchor

All the people in Porthaven loved old Trethscot the sailor, especially Wendy, Harry, Tamsin and George. He had left the navy many years ago but they loved listening to his tales about the sea.

In the summer holidays they would listen to his amazing stories. They heard about the time he fell overboard and was nearly eaten by sharks and about the time his ship caught fire and how the sailors put it out. There was no end to the stories he had to tell.

'I loved the sea,' he would say. 'If I had my life again I would do the same again. But, you know, the best part was coming home after months away at sea – to come into port and see the houses and the steeples of Porthaven again. Among the crowds who came to welcome us home, I could see my mum and dad and all my friends. It was like heaven. When we dropped the anchor, I knew I was home again with all the folks I loved. But now I am old and they are gone.'

When old Trethscot died the church was full for his funeral. Commodore Rawlings read the lesson and the minister paid tribute to Trethscot's service in the navy.

Outside there were many flowers left by friends, with a card on each bunch. One card had a picture of a ship, another of waves and the sea – and there were many others. They all carried similar messages, such as: 'Goodbye Trethscot. We will miss you.'

One bunch of flowers with a card was from Wendy, Harry, Tamsin and George which said:

'Dear Sailor Trethscot, Welcome home – happy again!'

And underneath their message they had drawn an anchor.

THE POINT

Home is where the heart is. That is where we find love, joy and happiness. This is the promise God makes to us, that we shall be happy with him for ever.

THE READING

Be glad when that happens, and dance for joy, because a great reward is kept for you in heaven. *Luke 6:23*

PRAYER

Father God,

Thank you for all the good things you give us now and for the joy and happiness you have planned for us in the future. *Amen.*

The Apple Trees

Len, Barbara, Gareth and Polly lived in Appleton. All you could see for miles around were apple trees, so there wasn't much to do all day in the summer. People said that it was beautiful, but really it was boring.

Sometimes, the children picked up the apples from the ground and fed them to Farmer Gleason's pigs. But after a while even that got a bit boring!

Then, one day, they came across an orchard, closed in by an iron gate and surrounded by high stone walls. On the gate there were warnings which read: DO NOT ENTER. TRESPASSERS WILL BE PROSECUTED.

'Let's climb over the wall and pinch some apples!' said Len.

'What for?' said Barbara. 'We've got millions of apples out here.'

'But this would be more fun!' said Len. 'Come on.'

And so they did. They helped each other to scale the walls. It was so exciting! Polly's heart was thumping. What if they got caught?

Then a man came out of his house. 'Who's out there?' he shouted. 'I can hear you!'

The children hid behind the trees. Even Gareth felt his heart pumping as the man came closer.

'Caught you! What are you doing here?' he said angrily.

Barbara was in tears. 'We came in to pinch some apples,' she said.

'Pinch apples!' said the man. 'Why did you want to do that? There are loads of apples out there.'

'It's my fault,' said Len. 'I told them to come in here. I thought it would be fun. It was just a dare.'

'Will we go to prison now?' Polly asked, crying.

The man began to laugh. 'Of course not,' he said, 'but let this be a lesson to you. Everyone knows that stealing is wrong and doing dares to please your friends could lead you into real danger.'

THE POINT

Sometimes we think that keeping up with friends is more important than doing the right thing.

READING

We pray to God that you will do no wrong – not in order to show that we are a success, but so that you may do what is right … *2 Corinthians 13:7*

PRAYER

Father God,

You know us and you love us. Please help us to be strong and do what is right. *Amen.*

The Ash Tip

On the last day of school, Margaret boasted that she was going on holiday to Santana and staying in a hotel with a swimming pool. Don said he was going to Sandaledo and Molly said she was going to the Costa Maria. All of them were going to places that were hot and were staying in hotels where there were swimming pools.

Mike went home and said: 'Mum, why can't we go on a holiday abroad, like everyone else?'

'Because we can't afford to!' she said. 'You'll have to go and stay with Auntie Nan in Caeraumen.'

Mike liked staying with Auntie Nan but Caeraumen wasn't really the best place for a holiday. It used to be a mining village and it wasn't even near the sea.

During their holiday, Margaret, Don and Molly enjoyed the first day or two swimming in the pools at their different places but soon got bored. Don said it was boring just swimming in the pool all day with no friends to play with – just grown-ups everywhere. His dad got cross with him and told him to stop complaining because the holiday had cost a lot of money.

Margaret and Molly were bored and saying the same things and getting on their parents' nerves.

Mike wasn't too happy either. 'There's nothing to do in Caeraumen,' he said.

'Well, just go out and find something to do,' Aunty Nan said. But there wasn't much to do. He went out for a walk and just wandered around – until he saw the ash tip! There he saw children sliding down the tip, one after another. Good job they weren't in their best clothes!

'What are you doing?' Mike asked.

'Practising for the Caeraumen Olympics,' said one of the boys. 'My name is Evan and I am the champion. The finals will be in ten days' time.'

'Can I join too?' said Mike.

'Why not?' said Evan.

And so Mike joined them. When Mike got back to Auntie Nan's she said: 'My goodness, you look a mess!'

But she wasn't cross – she never was. 'You'd better get into the bath and I shall wash your clothes.'

Later that night, as Mike was drinking his cocoa before bed, he told her all about the ash tip and how he was going to compete in the downhill sliding Olympics in ten days' time.

'Then I'd better find you some old clothes!' she said.

Mike joined his new friends every day. Evan showed him how to slide. After days of excitement and fun the great day came – the final!

Evan won again but Mike came second, so they gave him a silver medal made from a milk top and a piece of ribbon. Mike was so proud. Second in the Caeraumen Olympics! Not bad for a first try.

Mike was really sorry to say goodbye to his new friends and Auntie Nan and wished he could stay on a bit longer.

On the first day of the new term Mr Reynolds asked the children if they had enjoyed the holidays.

'It was all right,' said Don, Margaret and Molly, without much enthusiasm.

'It was fantastic!' said Mike.

THE POINT

Having everything you want doesn't always make you happy, but friendship does.

READING

Meanwhile these three remain: faith, hope and love; and the greatest of these is love. *1 Corinthians 13:13*

PRAYER

Father God,

Thank you for all my friends. Help me to be loving and kind to everybody.

Amen.

The Ballet Dancers

Celia, Polly, Samantha and Poppy used to go to ballet lessons in the village hall together on Friday evenings. Imagine their excitement when Miss Farrell announced that Lady Carlton was coming in November to see them dance. She said that if any of them were really special they might win a place in the Carlton Ballet School and even end up on the stage!

They worked very hard after hearing that. Miss Farrell gave them extra lessons and they all encouraged each other. They were all very nervous when Lady Carlton came, but they did well.

'You were all excellent,' she said. 'I can take three of you.'

Poppy wasn't one of those chosen and all the others who missed out were just as upset as she was. But you can't get everything you want in life and Poppy went on to become a carer in a nursing home.

One night there was a special programme on TV – The Carlton Ballet Company performing *La Fostoria*, by the new composer Salvatore Samprosi.

Everyone wanted to see it in the nursing home so Poppy arranged chairs round the TV. Mrs Benson couldn't see very well, so Poppy wheeled her to the front. Poppy was excited because she knew that her three friends from her schooldays would be dancing. And it was brilliant – the lights, the costumes and the orchestra were superb. She could see Celia, Polly and Samantha dancing on the stage and felt so proud of them.

When the performance finished the audience stood to their feet and applauded for more than ten minutes. All the dancers were given huge bouquets of flowers. It was wonderful!

Poppy put her arms round Mrs Benson. 'I knew three of the dancers,' she said. 'We went to ballet school together. I might have been out there with them, but I wasn't chosen.'

'This may sound rather selfish on my part,' said Mrs Benson, 'but I'm glad you weren't chosen and that you care for me.'

THE POINT

We all have gifts and even though some of them might not seem important they are all worthwhile and needed.

READING

We know that in all things God works for good … *Romans 8:28*

PRAYER

Father God,

You love each one of us and want us to be happy. Help us to use the gifts you have given to us to make the world a happier place. *Amen.*

The Bin Bags

Martha Higgins didn't have much money and she had to look after her four children – Andy, Kate, Don and Gina. So every day she went to cook and clean for Mr Felton, who lived down the road.

On Saturdays the children helped their mum to clean the whole house from top to bottom. It was hard work and Mr Felton didn't pay them very much because, as he said, he wasn't all that well off himself.

Even so, Martha was grateful. They earned enough to buy second-hand clothes and usually a chicken for Sunday lunch.

One day Mr Felton decided he needed to go away and have a good holiday, but he had a problem. He was very, very rich. In fact, he had lots of money, which he kept under the carpet in his bedroom. He thought to himself: 'What if burglars come when I am away and find my money under the carpet? What if Martha and the children decide to spring-clean and lift up the carpet in my bedroom? Then they would know that I am rich and I would have to pay them more money! It could happen.'

Then Mr Felton came up with a great idea. 'I'll hide all my money in bin bags and put them in the garage. No burglar would ever think of looking into rubbish bins to find money.'

It was a brilliant idea!

So before he left, Mr Felton put all his money in black plastic bin bags, covered the money with waste paper and empty cans and piled them up in his garage.

'No one will ever think of looking there for my money,' he thought, and off he went. He had a wonderful holiday – wining and dining in the most expensive hotels. On the last day he realised he'd spent all the money he had taken with him, but that didn't worry him. 'I've got lots more at home in the garage,' he thought.

When he got home Martha and the children were waiting for him. They were so proud. 'While you were away,' they said, 'we gave your house a thorough spring clean. We cleaned the carpets, scrubbed the kitchen, washed the walls, polished the staircase and tidied up your garden.'

Mr Felton was very pleased. 'Thank you,' he said, looking around. 'You have done more than I could ever want. I am going to give each of you £1 more for the extra work you've done!'

'And what's more,' said Kate, eagerly, 'we cleaned out your garage and got rid of all those smelly bin bags you left there!'

Mr Felton nearly fainted. 'But that's where I keep my money. You've thrown it all away,' he cried. 'Everything I have. That's where I hid all my money! Now I have nothing!'

Martha and the children were horrified. 'Oh, Mr Felton, we are sorry, we didn't know. We'll come and clean and look after you for nothing from now on,' they cried.

Mr Felton looked at the tears in Martha's eyes and how upset the children were. Then he realised how much love and care the whole family had shown to him, and he began to laugh.

'I'm glad you got rid of those bin bags,' he said. 'You've made a lonely man very happy.'

THE POINT

Love and care are more important than anything we possess.

READING

I have told you this so that my joy may be in you and that your joy may be complete. My commandment is this: love one another, just as I love you. *John 15: 11-12*

PRAYER

Father God,

You love us. Thank you for your love and for the care we give and get from others. Help us to see that this is more precious than all the things we think will make us happy. *Amen.*

The Bugs and the Dragonflies

Brian, Fred, Sandra and Lynne were little bugs who lived with their friends at the bottom of a swampy pool. It was dark and muddy but, even so, they were happy together.

Every now and then one of the little bugs' friends would climb up a reed to see what lay above. Whoever was climbing would say: 'I'll be back soon and tell you what it's like when I come back.'

But they never did come back. Sandra and Lynne went up as well – but they never came back. All the other bugs did the same. Soon, only Brian and Fred were left at the bottom of the pool.

Brian said to Fred: 'All the other bugs have climbed up the reed but have never come back – even Sandra and Lynne. You go up and I'll wait for you here, but promise me you'll come back and tell me what you find.'

'I promise you,' said Fred, and up he went.

When Fred got to the top of the reed he found himself on a beautiful blue pond. The sun shone down on him. He felt warm. Then his body began to warm, to grow longer, change colour and sprout wings!

Sandra, Lynne and all the other dragonflies came to greet him. 'Welcome home,' they said. 'You've now become a dragonfly like us! Let's show you around!'

Fred, the new dragonfly, had a wonderful day, flying round. He saw flowers and trees, birds and bees – things he never imagined existed when he was at the bottom of the pool.

He had such a good time that he forgot completely about Brian down below in the murky pond. Then he remembered. 'I must go back and tell Brian what it's like up here,' he said, and he flew down to the pond.

But when he got down to the reed he found he couldn't get back. He was changed. He was too big and he had wings. He couldn't climb back down. He felt so sad for poor little Brian, all on his own down there, but there was nothing he could do but pray for him.

Next day there was a ripple by the reed. Out popped Brian the bug. The sun shone, his body grew, changed colour and he sprouted wings. Everyone came to greet him – Fred, Sandra, Lynne and all his friends. 'We're sorry we couldn't come back and tell you,' they said.

Brian, the dragonfly, looked round – amazed and delighted.

'It doesn't matter any more,' he said. 'We're all together again and I've never been so happy.'

THE POINT

God loves us and has made us to be happy with him for ever.

READING

However, as the scripture says: 'What no one ever saw or heard, what no one ever thought could happen, is the very thing God prepared for those who love him.' *1 Corinthians 2:9*

PRAYER

Father God,

You love and care for us. May we your children enjoy our friendship here together and be happy with you for ever in heaven. *Amen.*

The Butterfly Farm

Uncle Arthur worked very hard on his market garden. He grew some carrots, turnips and potatoes but most of all … cabbages. A lorry used to come every day and take away boxes of cabbages for the markets. Larry, Emma, Ned and Martha used to help him.

One day Uncle Arthur had to go away for two weeks so he asked the children to look after his market garden. It wasn't much to ask. The carrots, turnips and potatoes could look after themselves but the cabbages needed more care. The children would have to pick off the caterpillars that would have otherwise eaten the leaves.

On the first day the children went out to the fields with buckets to pick up the caterpillars, but they didn't like that at all! The caterpillars were so slimy! They simply couldn't do a job like that, even though Uncle Arthur had promised to give them something when he returned.

When he did return he was very cross. All the cabbages had been eaten by the caterpillars. All his cabbages were ruined. The children said they were sorry, but explained that they didn't like picking up the caterpillars.

Next day Uncle Arthur sat on the veranda overlooking his ruined cabbage field. Then, suddenly, thousands of butterflies rose up from the ground. Uncle Arthur was amazed. He had never seen anything so beautiful.

The children came and sat by him. 'Aren't they beautiful?' they said.

'That is really wonderful,' said Uncle Arthur. 'Those caterpillars have turned into beautiful butterflies. That's what I'll do with my cabbages from now on.'

And so people come from all around to see Uncle Arthur's Butterfly Farm. The children still help him – explaining to the visitors how little caterpillars who can just about crawl turn into beautiful butterflies that can fly around all day, their beautiful wings reflecting the bright sunlight.

THE POINT

In this life, we can only glimpse the wonders of God's creation. In the next, we shall see things as they really are.

READING

I consider that what we suffer at this present time cannot be compared at all with the glory that is going to be revealed to us. *Romans 8:18*

PRAYER

Father God,

You have filled our world with beautiful things. Help us to protect and care for your creation. *Amen.*

The Doorbell

Granny Webber was just going to bed at 9 p.m., when the doorbell rang. She struggled up from her armchair, but when she got to the door there was no one there. Ten minutes later she heard the bell again, but there was no one there. Now she was frightened. Ten minutes later, it rang again. No one was there. This time she was really frightened. She got to bed but couldn't sleep, because she was so afraid, and so she phoned her son, Matt.

Matt thought she was just imagining things but agreed to go and stay with her and take along Linda, his daughter. Just as they were helping Granny Webber to bed the doorbell rang. Matt rushed out but there was nobody there. It happened again ten minutes later. Again, no one was there. Ten minutes later it rang again, but again nobody was there. Now Linda was really scared.

From then on the family took it in turns. Matt went one night with Linda, and then Mum went with Gary and Hannah the other. Every night the doorbell rang but on each occasion there was nobody there.

Granny was frightened. They even had to call the doctor to give her tablets. Matt was exhausted after working in the shop all day, and Mum was tired after nursing in the hospital. Hannah was very frightened and thought it might be a ghost. It happened every night. No one could sleep.

After a week of this, the doorbell rang again on Friday night. Matt rushed to the door. There was nobody there. He looked around. There was no sign of anybody. Then he heard a rustle in the bushes near the garden gate. He tiptoed to the bushes, trying not to make a sound.

Then he saw them! There was Michael Rafferty and his gang hiding in the bushes. 'Come out!' he shouted. Out from the bushes came the four scruffy boys, grinning from ear to ear.

'Why have you been ringing my mum's doorbell every night?' Matt demanded to know.

'We were just having fun,' laughed Michael. 'We didn't mean any harm.'

'Well,' said Matt. 'It wasn't funny for any of us. Granny was so frightened we had to call the doctor. We are all sick and tired of coming here every night.'

The boys looked shocked. 'We're sorry,' they said. 'We didn't mean to hurt anyone. We won't do it again.'

THE POINT

We don't want to hurt other people; but what seems like a bit of fun can be very frightening to others.

READING

Do for others just what you want them to do for you. *Luke 6:31*

PRAYER

Father God,

You give us love and happiness. Help us to be careful that our games and fun do not hurt others. *Amen.*

The Family of Rats

Mr and Mrs Edwards lived at Avonmore House – number 16 on Green Lane. They had two cats, two dogs and four children – Basil, Pearl, Wayne and Donna.

The Edwards loved to keep their house prim and proper, which they did. Even the cats and dogs had their own special places and bowls in the house.

The children brushed their teeth every morning and evening and had a shower every day. Everything had to be clean. The carpets were hoovered every day and the food bowls for the cats and dogs were kept clean and sparkling.

But then, things went wrong. The cups that had been left ready for breakfast were all over the floor and there were coffee stains on the carpet.

The cats and the dogs grew thinner, even though the children had measured out the same amount of food that they needed. Even the bin bags which Mum tied up so well were torn open, and there were used cartons all over the floor.

The answer was obvious. It was Grandad. He was getting a bit forgetful and probably got up hungry and thirsty in the night, drinking the coffee dregs and looking around for something to eat – even from the bowls. Maybe the time had come for him to go into a home, where he would be properly looked after.

Everyone was sorry the day he had to leave. Mike Shannon, his friend from next door who worked for the health authority, came round with a box of chocolates and to say goodbye. As Mike chatted to Grandad he looked at the edge of the carpet and said: 'How long have you had rats?'

Mum was shocked. 'Rats!' she said. 'How do you know we've got rats?'

Mike said: 'I can see their droppings on the edge of the carpet and there is a smell in here. I'll have a look round for you.' He did so and then said, 'Ah yes! There! There! There! No wonder you've had such trouble! I think there is a family of them somewhere.'

Just then the taxi arrived to take Grandad away to the home. Mr Edwards paid the taxi driver and told him he wasn't needed after all.

'I'm sorry, Dad,' he said. 'We thought it was you, but we were wrong. We thought that you needed more help than we could give you. So it's all right, Dad. You can stay with us.'

The children were delighted and gave Grandad a big hug.

'Thank you,' said Grandad, 'but I still don't understand why you wanted to me to go to a home.'

'We'll never make a mistake like that again,' said Mum.

THE POINT

Don't jump to conclusions and blame others.

READING

My dear friend, do not imitate what is bad, but imitate what is good. Whoever does good belongs to God; whoever does what is bad has not seen God. *3 John 1:11*

PRAYER

Father God,

We are your children and you love us. Help us always to follow your teaching. *Amen.*

The Final Whistle

When Woodford and Andale turned up at the cup final the ref didn't. He was ill. Both schools agreed that Mr Gibson from Woodford should be referee and Mr Murphy and Mr Hamilton from Andale would run the line. That seemed fair.

Woodford and Andale had never been in the final before and all three teachers were desperate to see their teams win. At half-time Woodford were 3-0 down. Mr Gibson made a few positional changes and told them they could still win!

And it worked! Benny (Christine) scored for Woodford. Ken (Liz) scored a second. That made it 3-2. After that, it was all Woodford. Andale defended with all their might and their goalkeeper, Mac, made four fantastic saves.

Mr Gibson and even the two linesmen knew it wouldn't last. Sooner or later Woodford would score again and then win the cup in extra-time.

The last ten minutes provided the most exciting action of the match. You could hear the shouts of parents, teachers and friends three streets away. Then Jack (Fiona) went past three Andale players and smashed the ball into the back of the net with the last kick of the game. That would have sent the final into extra-time!

'No goal,' said Mr Gibson. 'Andale have won the match 3-2.'

Some of the crowd were angry. Even Mr Murphy and Mr Hamilton were bewildered. It wasn't off-side and it seemed a perfectly good goal to them.

'No,' said Mr Gibson. 'The goal is disallowed.'

So Andale took the cup but felt, perhaps, they didn't deserve it. But that was the ref's decision.

Everyone clapped the disappointed Woodford team as they got their losers' medals. Then Mr Gibson addressed the teams and crowd. He said: 'Jack's (Fiona's) goal was on-side and the best I've ever seen, but a few seconds before the ball went in I had blown the whistle for full-time, but you didn't hear the whistle. I could have given the goal and no one would have known – but isn't it better to come second by doing your best, than coming first by cheating?'

THE POINT

Being honest and fair is better than getting what you want by cheating other people.

READING

Do for others just what you want them to do for you. *Luke: 6:31*

PRAYER

Father God,

You love us and we are all your children. Help us to be honest and fair with everyone we meet and to be glad to share our fun, play and happiness with others. *Amen.*

The Firefighter

James, Diana and Lorna went to the palace to watch their dad receive the Medal of Bravery. Dad was a firefighter who had saved many lives in a big blaze.

Tim went too, but he was too little to understand. However, he knew his dad must be a hero for all the fuss the people were making.

Mum tried to explain. 'Your dad,' she said, 'was very brave. He saved lots of lives in a fire even though he was in great danger. That's why he's been given this medal, even though he doesn't want one. We are all very proud of him.'

Dad's mum couldn't go to the palace to watch the ceremony, so they had a party next day. She wanted, at least, to see the medal. She was so proud of her son.

At the party, James, Diana and Lorna played with their friends from next door. Little Tim played with his friend, Andy, in the hut at the bottom of the garden.

After the party everybody came together to see the medal, except Tim and Andy, who were still playing and wouldn't understand what it was all about anyway.

Dad went to get his medal from indoors, but it had gone! It had disappeared! Maybe it had been stolen! They searched everywhere.

Then Dad said: 'It doesn't matter. I didn't really want a medal. I am just so pleased I was able to save other people's lives. Now I'd better get Tim. It's time he was getting ready for bed.'

When Dad got to the hut he saw Andy placing the medal on little Tim. 'Wear this medal,' he was saying. 'You are wonderful and brave!'

Dad wasn't cross. He just said: 'Why did you take my medal? We've been looking for it everywhere.'

'We were only playing,' said little Tim. 'I just wanted to be like you.'

And Tim got the biggest hug he'd ever had in his life.

THE POINT

Jesus is our hero; if we follow him then we will grow into loving, caring people.

READING

… the Son can do nothing on his own; he does only what he sees his Father doing. What the Father does, the Son also does. *John 5:19*

PRAYER

Father God,

Thank you for sending us Jesus. Please help us to be as loving and caring as he was. *Amen.*

The Flower Show

St Mary's church in Greenwoods had seven stained-glass windows – three on one side and three on the other, and a very big one behind the main altar. Every year they had a flower show and the ladies picked flowers from their gardens to arrange before each window. The best arrangement went in front of the big stained-glass window.

The rector told them that their flowers would be like a present – a prayer of thanksgiving to God.

Mrs Camber-Wright was sure that hers would be the best and would take pride of place before the big window, but so did Mrs Melrose-Vivian and Mrs Calder-Pierce.

Lady Lacy-Lambert had other ideas. She had the best garden in the village and a very good gardener. 'I shall make the best flower arrangement this year,' she thought. 'And mine will be displayed before the big window, for everyone to see.'

Hannah, Gerry, Frank and Debbie wanted to make a flower arrangement but their mum said: 'Don't be silly. We haven't even got a garden – but we shall go on Sunday to see the lovely flower displays the others have made.'

'Let's make our own and bring it to the church – after all, the rector said it's only a prayer,' said Hannah.

So they did. They picked foxgloves, buttercups, daisies and grasses. The colours were beautiful.

When they got to the church Rector Newton was already placing the flowers before the windows. Lady Lacy-Lambert was furious that hers were put near to the back.

So were all the other women, when their flowers were placed by the side windows. The main space in front of the large window remained empty. The children came in and Rector Newton placed their flowers in front of the main window.

He said: 'These flowers the children picked are their prayer of love and praise to God. The other arrangements were not.'

Even Lady Lucy got the point.

THE POINT

Little things we do for God are better than great things we do for ourselves.

READING

Well, whatever you do … do it all for God's glory. *1 Corinthians 10:31*

PRAYER

Father God,
All that we have, we give to you, but most of all we give you our love.
Amen.

The Gold Watch

Pat, Emily, Mike and Josie went away for two weeks for summer camp. They had a good time but missed their mum and dad. On the last day they had run out of money and just had £5 between them – only just enough for a bag of chips and one ice cream each. They went off to spend all they had left. On the way they passed a stall where a man was selling gold watches.

'Gold watches!' he shouted. '£5 each. A bargain at the price! Today only! Get one now!'

Emily said: 'Let's get a present for Dad. A gold watch! He'd love that! It's much better to give Dad a present than spend the money we've got left on chips and ice cream.'

And so they did.

The man smiled at them and said: 'Don't ask me where they came from!' Then he wrapped up the watch in a box and told them not to open it until they got home. And so they did.

Dad was delighted. 'I've never had a gold watch before!' he said. He was so proud of his watch that he looked at it every ten minutes to tell the time.

Then one day Dad had to go away for a week on work. He accidentally left the watch on the windowsill. Pat saw it and said: 'It's stopped! It's not working! Let's go to Fred the jeweller and get it mended before Dad comes back home.'

And so they did.

They told Fred the jeweller that the watch was very precious. In fact, pure gold! Fred opened up the watch and began to laugh! 'There's nothing inside,' he said. 'You've been conned! It isn't gold – just enamel paint! This watch isn't worth anything!'

When Dad got home Pat said: 'You knew all the time the watch didn't work. Why did you just pretend that you thought it was gold?'

Dad said: 'Yes, I knew, but it was worth much more than gold to me, because you gave it to me.'

THE POINT

Any prayer, thought, word or deed we give to God our Father is more precious than silver and gold.

READING

Jesus answered, 'Love the Lord your God with all your heart, with all your soul, and with all your mind.' *Matthew 22:37*

PRAYER

Father God,

Everything we have is given by you. Take back our lives as an offering to you. *Amen.*

The Hole in the Sand

Professor Littlebrain lived in a house overlooking Sandy Beach. His name was misleading, because he had a brilliant brain and had discovered many things about nature and the world. But still he wasn't happy. He wanted to know the answer to everything, such as how the universe began and what was there before.

So every day he walked along the beach trying to think of the answers to all his questions. As he did, he often walked past Cecilia, Ted, Fleur and Phillip, playing in the sand as Mum and Dad looked on. Each had a little bucket and they raced to the sea and back to collect water, to fill up a pool they had dug in the sand.

That was another question that puzzled the professor. Why were little children running back and forth from the sea all day? And why were they pouring buckets of water into their little hole? And so one day he asked them.

'Can't you see?' Ted answered. 'We are going to empty all the sea and pour it into the hole we have made.'

The professor laughed. 'You can't do that,' he said. 'The sea is too big and great and your little hole is too small to take it all in.'

'Just like the universe,' said Fleur. 'It is so great and wonderful. Our little brains are too small to take it all in. We can't know everything.'

'But there must be a reason for everything,' said the professor, 'and I must find out.'

'But only God can tell you that!' said Phillip.

THE POINT

Even though we may be clever, only God can tell us why the world was made and why we are here – for love, and to live and be happy with God for ever.

READING

When I see the moon and the stars; all the wonders you have made, it makes me think why you made me as well. Then I know you made the world for us. *Paraphrase of Psalm 8*

PRAYER

Father God,

You made the world and all its wonders just for us, so that we could be happy for ever. Help us to see your love in the world today. *Amen.*

The Lifeguard

At last, Alice, Duncan, Chris and Jean were on holiday in Sandown. They looked out of the hotel window and saw the sea. It was a lovely, hot day. The sky was blue and the sea looked calm and inviting. They couldn't wait to get into the water. Then Dad saw the red flag on the beach.

'That means it's very dangerous,' Dad said, 'so you can play on the sand but you can't swim.'

The children played on the beach and made sandcastles. It was hot. The sea still looked so calm and inviting. 'We could splash and paddle by the edge,' they said, 'but not go out too far.'

They took their things and went nearer to the water's edge.

Then Duncan began to wade out a bit further – but not too far. The water was beautiful, cool and clear. Then he had a little swim – but not too far. The water was just up to his knees.

'It's lovely!' he shouted. 'Come and join me!'

'No!' said Alice. 'We were told not to.'

Duncan was having a great time. He swam a little further and shouted: 'Come and join me.'

Then suddenly he felt a current underneath, dragging him down and further away from the shore. No matter how hard he tried, he couldn't swim back to the shore.

Then from a hut nearby came a lifeguard. He got to Duncan just when he thought he was drowning, picked him up and brought him back on to the beach.

From further up the beach Mum and Dad saw what had happened and came running down. Mum just wanted to cuddle Duncan in her arms and thank the brave lifeguard. 'Wait,' said Dad, as he saw the lifeguard. 'This will do him good. '

The lifeguard was towering over Duncan and shouting at all the children. He seemed to be very, very angry.

'Didn't you see the red flag?' he shouted. 'Never, never, never do that again! Do you understand! Do you understand!' he screamed over and over again. 'Never, never, never do that again!'

Duncan and the others were near to tears and glad when the angry lifeguard left them. Dad couldn't be angry now because he thought they'd had enough, and Mum was just glad to put her arms round Duncan and cuddle him.

'That man was really horrible,' said Jean, running up to Dad. 'He really frightened me.'

'That man,' said Dad, 'saved Duncan's life. He was angry because he wanted you to be safe. I think we'd better go over and thank him.'

But when they got to the hut, the man had gone.

THE POINT

We must always obey warning signs and safety rules. God loves us and wants us to be safe and happy.

READING

All those who obey his word are people whose love for God has really been made perfect. *1 John 2:5*

PRAYER

Father God,

You love us and want us to be safe and happy. Help us to obey those who care for us. *Amen.*

The Little Fellow

Jackie O'Connor was a skinny little fellow and he wasn't very tall, either. His brother Brendan was huge and he was captain of Carville School rugby team. Jackie wanted to play in the team but he was far too small.

'Don't worry,' said Mr Fleming, the sports teacher. 'We can't be good at everything.'

His sisters, Amy and Sophie, were really good at running, but Jackie wasn't. He couldn't keep up with them. 'Never mind,' said Miss Phillips. 'We can't be good at everything.'

'But I'm not good at anything,' Jackie thought.

When they went on holiday to Uncle Frank's farm, Brendan played rugby with him but didn't throw the ball too hard. The girls raced with him but didn't run too fast.

Then one day Uncle Frank took them to a field to have a ride on his horse, Lazy Lizzie. Brendan got on first, but no way was that horse going to move with a big lump like that on her back. Then the girls had a try, but she still wouldn't move.

'That's why I call her Lazy Lizzie,' said Uncle Frank. 'She doesn't do anything.'

Then Jackie had a go. Lazy Lizzie began to move. First a walk, then a trot, and then she started to gallop. She couldn't feel little Jackie on her back but somehow she knew he was there.

Together they galloped round the field. Jackie squealed with delight.

Mum screamed in horror. 'Stop! Stop!' she shouted. 'This is dangerous!'

But Jackie couldn't hear her.

Jackie and Lazy Lizzie went round and round the field. Then they raced towards Mr Maguire's field and jumped over the hedge. Mr Maguire was furious, but then Jackie and Lizzie jumped back over the hedge.

They all scolded Jackie, saying: 'Never do that again.'

Later that year Lazy Lizzie had a foal and they called her Lucky Lady Lizzy, after her mum. Every year the children came back to see how she had grown and to have a ride. Even Mr Maguire didn't mind them jumping over his hedges.

Six years later, the crowds at the National Gold Cup race meeting roared, and millions watched on television as Jackie O'Connor, in his yellow and blue, raced past the winning post on Lucky Lady Lizzy!

Frank Murphy received the cup as the owner of the horse. Paddy Maguire got a silver plate as the trainer. Jockey Jackie, as they now called him, received the golden disc. Brendan and the girls looked on with pride.

'I wish I could be up there with him now, 'said Brendan.

'Well now,' said Dad, 'you can't be good at everything.'

THE POINT

We all have gifts and all of them are different.

READING

… but each one has a special gift from God, one person this gift, another one that gift. *1 Corinthians 7:7*

PRAYER

Father God,

Thank you for all the gifts you have given to us. Help us to use them to help to make people happy. *Amen.*

The Little Table

Every evening Basu, Ravi, Amela and Harsha sat down with Mum, Dad and Grandad Narayan for a lovely meal together. Grandad Narayan was very, very old and sometimes used to spill his rice over the table, so they gave him a big bowl. Ravi liked sitting next to Grandad, even though he still dropped bits of rice and curry over the table, in spite of the bowl they had given him.

Of course when the Narayan family entertained special guests for dinner, like the district governor and his wife, they couldn't let Grandad be there. Instead, they brought a nice bowl of rice and curry to his room, so he could eat alone on a little table in the corner. In that way, he could spill his curry and no one would see and it could be easily cleaned up when the important guests had gone home.

Ravi didn't like important people coming because he liked Grandad being with them, even if he did spill rice over the table. But grown-ups knew what was best, so that was the way it was.

The children loved going to the village school, especially on Fridays, when they had woodwork class. At the end of term they could take home the things they had made.

One Friday Basu came home and gave Grandad a lovely tray he had made for him. Amela gave him a big wooden spoon with a flower painted on it. Little Harsha gave him a paper fan she had made.

Ravi didn't bring anything for Grandad because he had made his gift for his father. It was a little table. Dad laughed.

'Thank you, Ravi,' he said. 'That's lovely! But why did you make a table? We already have plenty of tables in the house and others in the shed.'

Full of love and pride, Ravi said: 'But I made this especially for you, for when you get old like Grandad.'

THE POINT

Everybody is important and everybody needs to be treated with dignity, love and respect.

READING

Show respect for old people and honour them. *Leviticus 19:32*

PRAYER

Father God,

Show us how to love and care for others in the same way that you love and care for us. *Amen.*

The Long Way Home

Abebi, Damasi, Adlila and Dalili had a day off from school, so they went on an adventure in the jungle. Soon they came across a lovely river and there on the riverbank they found an old raft.

'Let's jump on this raft,' said Dalili, 'and go out on the river. We can paddle with our hands.'

And so they did.

Mr Odifin was passing by on the hill above.

'Come back,' he shouted. 'That river is dangerous! ' But the children didn't hear him.

Sure enough, Mr Odifin was right. When the children got to the middle of the river the current became stronger and swept the raft downstream. Faster and faster they went for miles and miles until they slowed down on a huge lake.

There, they paddled ashore.

'We're lost,' said Abebi. 'We will never get home. Mum and Dad will be crying for ever.'

Dalili said: 'Of course we will get back. We will walk back even if it takes us days.'

So off they went. But it was much harder than they had expected. Adlila was only small and they had to take it in turns to carry her. They came across a snake pit right in their path.

'Hiss, hiss, hiss!' went the snake.

Damasi led them along a narrow path over the pit. It seemed to take hours. One slip and they would be lost.

Next, they came across a river that was full of crocodiles and they had to walk for miles until they came to a waterfall where they could get across. In the day they ate any nuts and fruit they could find and at night they huddled together under the trees.

At home the villagers had given up hope. Mum and Dad were crying.

On the third day, after climbing over a mountain, the children saw before them a great, barren plain. Damasi jumped for joy and said: 'I know this place. I've been here before! We are not far from home! Look, there's a rough road that will take us back to the village! We could get there by tonight!'

But the others were too tired by now and just wanted to lie down and give up.

'Come on,' said Damasi. 'We can get there if we try.'

And so they did. But it was hard and the road was rough.

At sunset they saw the village and then their father's house and all the people crying.

'We're home!' Damasi shouted! 'We got back home!'

And so the village danced all night while all four children slept safe and sound.

THE POINT

If someone has set his mind on coming to the place of his heart's desire, danger and rough roads won't stop him.

READING

We are often troubled, but not crushed; sometimes in doubt, but never in despair; there are many enemies, but we are never without a friend; and though badly hurt at times, we are not destroyed. *2 Corinthians 4:8-9*

PRAYER

Father God,

When we are unhappy, help us to remember that you love us and want us to be happy. *Amen.*

The Lottery

Matt and Maggie McGregor had a very happy family but they were always short of money. Barry and Carmen loved swimming, Bert and Karen loved drama. Mum and Dad found it hard to pay for all their out-of-school activities, but they managed, even though it sometimes meant having only baked beans on toast for tea.

Dad said: 'If only we could make more money, we could be really happy.'

And so they bought a lottery ticket every week. They always picked the same numbers: all the children's birthdays – 6, 14, 21 and 28, and Mum's and Dad's ages – 39 and 45 (even though they didn't like to say they were).

Dad worked hard at the office. Mum was the school secretary and during her lunch break she did their shopping and bought the lottery ticket at the supermarket. But their numbers never came up.

One Wednesday evening Mum was late. She had been busy all day and had to stay on for the governors' meeting. At home, the family watched the lottery draw on television. The numbers came out. Fourteen was first.

'That's one of ours,' said Dad.

Thirty-nine was next. 'Another of our numbers,' said Dad.

Then came six. Dad sat forward and started to get excited. 'Yes!' he shouted.

Twenty-eight was next. 'I can't believe it,' he said. 'Unbelievable!'

Everyone was holding their breath, just waiting for the next number. Twenty-eight or forty-five would do. Then forty-five came out. It was unbelievable! They all jumped up and down.

'Please! Please! Please!' Dad prayed. 'Make the next number twenty-eight!'

And then out popped the next ball – number twenty-eight!

They all jumped for joy and danced around the house for half an hour. 'We're rich! Rich! Rich!' they sang. 'Millions, millions, millions!'

When Mum came in at eight o'clock, looking very tired, she wondered what all the excitement was about and why they were all dancing.

'We're rich, rich, rich! 'they chanted. 'We've won the lottery! Now we can be happy!'

Mum's face went white and she buried her hands in her face.

'I'm so sorry,' she cried. 'I was so busy I forgot to buy a ticket this week. You haven't won anything.'

All went silent for a while. 'Don't cry,' said Carmen. 'We've still got you and Dad and everything we had before.'

'And I've still got you and all your love!' Dad shouted. 'Money can't buy that!'

That night they still ate beans on toast, but what a lovely time they had together.

THE POINT

Money does not buy happiness.

READING

Don't let people set their hopes on money but on God who gives us true riches and happiness. *Paraphrase of 1 Timothy 6:17*

PRAYER

Father God,

You love us and give us everything we need. Help us to be happy with what we have. *Amen.*

The Lovely Day

Every year Grandad went to visit the Daltons for a week, and this year Mr Dalton wanted to make it a really special week. He had it all planned out.

On Monday, when Grandad arrived, they'd have a special meal together. On Tuesday they would take him to hear Carlo Pannetti at the opera house – Grandad loved music. On Wednesday they would go to see United play City in the big cup game – Grandad loved football and had supported City since he was a boy. On Thursday they would go to the Pandover Gardens, because Grandad loved flowers. Then finally, on Friday – weather permitting – they would have a day at Seaford, because Grandad loved to sit on the beach.

But then everything went wrong.

Carlo Pannetti's concert was cancelled at the last moment, so they stayed at home playing card games together.

'Don't be sad, Grandad,' said Chris, putting his arms round him. 'You'll see the football match tomorrow.' But that went wrong as well. They were too late. All the tickets were sold.

So they stayed at home and played card games together. 'Don't be disappointed, Grandad,' said Angela. 'Tomorrow we're going to see the Pandover Gardens.' But Dad had forgotten it was Bank Holiday and the gardens were closed to host a concert. So they all stayed at home and played card games together.

On Friday they were all ready for a day at the seaside but it rained and rained and rained – so they had to spend another day playing card games together.

Frank said: 'We shall miss you tomorrow when you leave.'

The next day the family all went to the bus station to see Grandad off. It was a beautiful day. The sun was shining and there wasn't a cloud in the sky. 'I'm sorry, Dad,' said Mr Dalton. 'Everything went wrong. And look – this is such a beautiful day. It's such a pity.'

'Every day is a beautiful day,' said Grandad as he waved goodbye. 'Especially if you have a family like mine, who still love you. Thank you for a wonderful week.'

THE POINT

Actions speak louder than words! Love is not just about doing things but being with your friends.

READING

Do all your work in love. *1 Corinthians 16:14*

PRAYER

Father God,

You love us and show us how to love others. Help us to love and care for everybody. *Amen.*

The Megastar

The news went round that Glitzy Megastar and his Flashlight Band were going to perform in the National Stadium – but you couldn't get tickets for love or money.

Donna, Tim, Jane and Eric wanted to go, but the tickets weren't available. And even if they had been, they wouldn't have been able to pay for them, because they were so expensive. But TV and radio had a competition for fans who could write the best line about the band. The prize was four free tickets for the concert – and Tim and his friends won!

After the concert they were so close to Glitzy Megastar that they were even able to touch him! Tim tried to get his autograph but Megastar's minder pushed him away.

'Glitzy Megastar doesn't sign autographs,' he said.

The children were disappointed but at least they could say they had seen and touched Glitzy Megastar and been to his concert.

The children grew up, moved abroad and had children of their own. Then one Easter they all came back together and had a family picnic in the city park. As they ate their lovely picnic they talked about the day they had seen the Megastar. Their children were fascinated to hear the story. They wished they could have seen the Megastar themselves.

While they were eating Tim noticed an old man with his little dog, picking up bits of food here and there, which people had left behind.

'Look at that poor old man,' he said. 'Let's invite him to join us.'

And so they did. The old man scoffed everything left over. He must have been very hungry and Tim felt sorry for him.

'How come you're so poor and lonely?' he said. 'Has no one ever given you a job?'

'Oh yes,' said the old man. 'I used to have a job and lots of money and friends. I thought it would never end. But then I spent it all and all my friends went away. They didn't want to know me any more.'

'What did you used to do? 'Angie asked, feeling very sorry for him.

'You wouldn't know,' he said. 'You're far too young. I used to sing in a band.'

'Glitzy Megastar?' said Tim.

'How did you know?' the old man asked.

'Because we saw you,' he said. 'We were there. So now, after all this time, will you sign your autograph for me?'

'What for?' said the old man. 'No one cares about me any more.'

'We do,' said Angie.

THE POINT

Love for others is more important than pride and fame.

READING

He has stretched out his mighty arm and scattered the proud with all their plans. He has brought down mighty kings from their thrones, and lifted up the lowly. *Luke 1:51–52*

PRAYER

Father God,

Everything we have comes from you. Let us care for all your children, share their joys when all goes well and still love them when all goes wrong and they need our friendship. *Amen.*

The Night the Lights Went Out

Orla, Conrad, Monica and David lived in a lovely house on Orchard Lane, just outside town. Dad had a very good job and gave them all they needed – TVs, DVD players and computers in every room! Dad didn't see them much because he had to work late every night and didn't want to be disturbed when he came home.

'After all,' he thought, 'I want to give my children the best – and that takes time and money.' But he always said good night to them before they went to bed.

Mum was also busy, too – every week she wrote an article for a fashion magazine which had to be ready for Monday. So most nights the family had meals that Mum had got ready in the microwave.

One night Mum and Dad were both working and the children were in their rooms using their computers when the lights went out. It was a power cut. Something had gone wrong! Then there was panic.

Dad couldn't work. Mum couldn't finish what she was writing. The children couldn't watch TV, listen to their music or use their computers.

Dad found some candles. They all sat together in the front room with nothing to do. Then Dad told them a story about when he was a boy living on a farm, and about the day he fell into a pig trough!

Everyone laughed!

'You never told us that before,' said Orla. Then Mum told them about the time Grandad got on the wrong train and landed up in Scotland!

'And that's not all,' she said, and told them more stories about the past that made them laugh.

Suddenly the lights came on again. The fault had been repaired. Everyone jumped for joy, because they could go back to their rooms, their computer games and their work!

'No,' Dad said. 'Switch off the lights just for now and let's carry on telling each other stories about ourselves.'

And as they did, he looked again at his lovely family and thought: 'Thank God the lights went out tonight.'

THE POINT
Love and sharing time together is better than anything else.

READING
And now I give you a new commandment: love one another. As I have loved you, so you must love one another. *John 13:34*

PRAYER
Father God,
You love us all. Let us share that love with you and with everyone we meet. *Amen.*

The Organist

Pastor David didn't have many people in the chapel on Sunday evenings, which was not surprising. The music was terrible! Old Auntie Nan played the organ but often got the notes wrong, what with her gammy right hand and her failing eyesight.

Linda, Nick, Ken and Owen made up the choir with their mums and dads but they weren't very good. Grandad Dan made it worse. He sang at the top of his voice but was always out of tune. But at least they did their best and wanted to sing praise and thanks to God.

Imagine Pastor David's delight when Sir Michael Landsman rang his door on a Tuesday evening and announced that he and his family had come to live in Riverside Village and were willing to offer them their services.

Sir Michael was a brilliant organist and had performed concerts all over Europe! His daughters, Elizabeth and Helena, played the oboe and cello and had been featured on national television.

The only problem was that Pastor David had to tell Auntie Nan that she had to go, which, in fact, didn't turn out as badly as he had expected. Auntie Nan was disappointed but thought it would be for the best.

News soon got round about the music at St Kit's chapel and people started to come back to church and they even formed a new choir under Sir Michael.

Then a great day came, when TV Enterprise chose St Kit's for *A Service of Holy Songs* to be broadcast throughout the country. Everyone came, even Lord and Lady Albright – the first time they had ever been seen there!

Sir Michael was brilliant and wore his music gown, which was very impressive. Grandad and the children gave out the hymn sheets but were told not to sing during the service, in case it spoilt the programme.

Pastor David was delighted. He'd never seen his church so full before!

Two days later Sir Michael came round to see Pastor David. 'I'm sorry,' he said. 'We're leaving. I have been appointed music professor at the Bach Academy and I can't turn that down. It has been nice living here and knowing you.'

The next Sunday the church was nearly empty again, but for Grandad Dan, Auntie Nan, the children and a few mums and dads. The music, once again, was terrible – even worse than before!

'I'm sorry,' said Auntie Nan. 'I got all the notes wrong. Grandad was out of tune and the children didn't sing very well either. I am sorry!'

'But we did try,' said Linda. 'We did try our best to sing our thanks to God.'

Pastor David looked round his chapel. It was no longer full. There were only the few faithful families and Grandad Dan, Auntie Nan and three old people praying in the corner.

'I'm really, really sorry,' said Auntie Nan again.

'I'm not, because you all want to be here to praise God,' said Pastor David.

THE POINT

Prayer, praise and love come from the heart. It is wonderful to have beautiful music and singing, but if it does not come from the heart then it does not praise God.

READING

Jesus answered, 'Love the Lord your God with all your heart, with all your soul, and with all your mind.' *Matthew 22:37*

PRAYER

Father God,

We thank you for all the good things you give us. Help us to love you more and more. *Amen.*

The Paramedic

Sandy, Jason, Karen and Barry Robson were very proud of Bob, their dad. Mrs Robson, their mum, was also very proud of Bob. He wasn't rich and he wasn't poor. He wasn't a doctor, but he could drive an ambulance and he helped people who were sick by getting them to hospital.

It was Sandy's birthday, and Bob was determined to give them all a treat – a meal together at the Caruana, where you had to book a week in advance in order to get a table. The children had never seen a place like it and Mr Caruana was even there at the entrance to greet them – as was his custom.

The waiter brought them the menu and Bob's face dropped when he saw the prices. 'I can't afford all this,' he thought, but he ordered the soup, which came with bread and olives.

Ten minutes later another group turned up. The waiters were all around them.

Barry became excited. He couldn't believe his eyes.

'That's Van Vergerhaus!' he said. 'City bought him from Radcliffe United for £8 million. And that's Silviano! United bought him from Castella for £12 million. That's Diego from Brazil!'

Barry certainly knew his football.

'I wish Dad was a famous footballer,' thought Jason, 'then we could come here every day and I could show off to my friends at school.'

Bob whispered to Mum: 'I made a mistake. We shouldn't have come here. I didn't realise it would be so expensive. We'll have our soup and then we can get them a pizza on the way home.'

The waiter came back. 'What would you like for your main course?' he asked.

'That's all!' said Bob. 'The soup was excellent. Now just bring us the bill, please.'

'Very well, sir,' said the waiter, looking down on them. Bob couldn't wait to pay the bill and get out as quickly as possible. By now, the place was filling up with stars from film and TV.

The waiter returned, not with the bill but with dishes of the most delicious food.

'I didn't order a second course,' said Bob.

Mr Caruana's orders,' said the waiter, looking down his nose at them. He is often quite generous to those in need.'

'Let's go,' said Bob. 'We don't need charity. I have my pride.'

'Eat it,' said Mum. 'Mr Caruana can afford it, even though we can't.'

Then they had ice cream, cheese and biscuits, and coffee and chocolate, before Mr Caruana eventually appeared.

'I hope you enjoyed your meal,' he said. 'It's not much but just my little way of saying thank you.'

'Thank you? For what?' said Bob.

Mr Caruana looked at the children and said: 'I'm glad your dad's a paramedic.' Then he looked around the restaurant and said: 'All this is mine, and I know all these famous faces – but I recognised you as soon as you came in. Two years ago I was in an accident and you saved my life. But for you, I wouldn't be here at all.'

'I don't remember that,' said Bob. But then he'd seen so many accidents.

'I'm glad my dad's a paramedic,' said Jason.

THE POINT

We often look up to people who are rich, famous and successful but often, those who care for us go unnoticed. Love and care are more important than fame.

READING

My commandment is this: love one another, just as I love you. *John 15:12*

PRAYER

Father God,

Being rich and famous doesn't matter. Help us just to love and help each other. *Amen.*

The Safari

Gathoni, Hafsa, Gasira and Haiba lived in the village of Kabala. Life was fun but sometimes hard, especially as they had to walk ten miles to the water well every day and all the way back with their buckets full (and heavy!).

About a hundred miles away the Connington-Trents were beginning their holiday of a lifetime at the Hotel Africana, in Ubatsi. The food and service there were magnificent. They had everything they needed.

On Thursday Mr Connington-Trent announced he was taking them all on a day trip to the middle of nowhere. He knew what he was doing because he had worked in Africa a few years previously and had done this before. He hired a four-wheel drive truck and filled it with everything they would need for the day – especially water.

The family had a wonderful day. They saw elephants, giraffes and lions. In the afternoon, they stopped at an open space and had a picnic of eggs, ham, fruit, cheese and cakes. The hotel had packed them a delicious lunch. But it was very hot and they drank all the water they had brought.

'We'd better get back soon,' said Dad. He turned on the ignition but the truck wouldn't start. 'No problem,' he said. 'I'll phone the hotel and they'll send someone out to fix it.' Then he found his mobile wasn't working either. They were stranded.

Mum was terrified. Kate, Justin, Greg and Pauline were frightened. They could sense that they were all in big trouble. Dad tried for hours to fix the engine but still nothing happened.

It was hot and they were thirsty – really, really thirsty.

'I'll walk back to Ubatsi,' said Dad, 'and get some help.'

'You'll never make it,' said Mum.

'Then what can we do?' he asked.

'I don't know,' said Mum.

Just then, they heard the sound of children's laughter and soon saw Gathoni, Hafsa, Gasira and Haiba coming up the track.

'We're saved!' said Dad. 'If these children survive here, so can we!' and the family all rushed forward to meet them.

'Water! Water!' he pleaded. 'Where can we find water?'

Hafsa laughed. 'There's a well just over there,' she said. 'There's plenty of water!'

'And food?' said Mum, anxiously. 'There must be a village nearby where we can get food.'

'Yes, come with us,' said Haiba. 'It's only ten miles away.'

'Only ten miles!' said the Connington-Trents.

'You'll make it if you try,' said Gathoni.

And they did!

After a little bread and fruit in Kabala Village that night Mr Nkkrubu said that he would walk to Ubatsi the next day and get them help.

Of course, it took several days before help arrived and they had to stay in Kabala eating just bread and fruit. The Connington-Trent children thought it was good fun. They made friends with the other children and even enjoyed walking each day to the well.

Mum was amazed at how the villagers lived and said to the children: 'I wonder how they survive on so little, when we have so much.'

THE POINT

Our world is rich but many people are poor. We can all help one another.

READING

If you have love for one another, then everyone will know that you are my disciples. *John 13:35*

PRAYER

Father God,

Thank you for all the gifts you give us, and help us to value them and share generously with others. *Amen.*

The Service Station

It was the most exciting day that the Newtons had ever shared. They were on their way to Spain for a holiday. They had saved up all year and everything was booked and paid for. They left early, because if they missed the plane they wouldn't get their money back and they wouldn't be able to have a different flight.

On the road to the airport Mr Newton kept making nasty remarks about the other drivers.

'Stop moaning,' said Mrs Newton. 'We're going on holiday. We should all be happy.'

So Mr Newton drove silently for the next ten minutes until four motorcycles overtook them.

'Look at them!' he shouted. 'Idiots! They should be off the roads. They care about no one but themselves!'

'Oh do stop it. Stop moaning,' said Mrs Newton. 'We're going on holiday and you're spoiling it.'

Later on they passed the bikers drinking tea at a roadside café in a lay-by.

'Good job – they're out of the way,' said Mr Newton.

'Please stop moaning,' said Mrs Newton. 'They can't be all that bad and they're not doing anybody any harm!'

A little further down the road Mr Newton stopped at Fairways Service Station to buy petrol. When he got back in the car it wouldn't start. He went back into the service station and queued up behind the others who were paying for petrol and buying papers. Time was running out. They might miss the plane!

'My car has broken down,' said Mr Newton. 'Can you help me?'

'Sorry sir,' said the man behind the till. 'We're a service station, not a garage. You'll have to phone the rescue service.'

'Then can I use your phone?' he pleaded. 'I've left my mobile at home.'

'Sorry, sir,' the man said. 'It's out of order.'

When Mr Newton went back and told the family, Frank, Helen, Jack and Kirsty burst into tears. They thought their holiday was in jeopardy.

Then the four motorcyclists came roaring into the station to fill up. 'That's all I need now,' said Mr Newton angrily.

But Kirsty thought they didn't look all that bad with their helmets off.

'What's wrong?' said one of them, seeing the children crying.

'Our car's broken down,' cried little Helen. 'We can't get to the airport now and we'll miss our holiday.'

'Let's have a look,' said the man, and he called over to his mate Harry to give a hand. They lifted up the bonnet and fiddled around with the engine inside.

'There,' he said. 'Give it a try.'

It worked!

'I am so grateful,' said Mr Newton, taking out his wallet. 'Can I give you something?'

'No! That's all right, mate,' said the biker. 'Glad to do you a favour.'

THE POINT

Don't judge people by their outward appearance.

READING

Stop judging by external standards, and judge by true standards. *John 7:24*

PRAYER

Father God,

Help us to see the good in others and be kind to everyone we meet. *Amen.*

The Soprano

Margaret had been bridesmaid at her mum's second marriage, when she married Eric. Afterwards her mum and Eric were going on honeymoon for a fortnight, so that they could have some time together.

It had been arranged that Margaret would stay with Eric's brother and family in Greenville, while they were away.

Greenville was lovely. Eric's brother and wife made Margaret very welcome. Their children – Clare, Laurie, Phillip and Agnes – made her feel welcome, too.

Eric's brother was a famous conductor. His wife was a very good pianist. Larry played the violin, Phillip played the clarinet, Agnes played the oboe and Clare had the most beautiful voice Margaret had ever heard.

The family were practising for the Greenville Children's Music Festival and Margaret was allowed to sit and listen to them every day, as long as she kept very, very quiet. Margaret loved to listen to them and she never missed a practice morning, noon or evening.

Margaret and Clare became great friends and went for walks together. Margaret said she loved hearing Clare sing but she didn't understand the words. 'That's because they're in Latin,' Clare said. 'Dad says you have to understand the words before you can sing them from your heart.'

Clare explained to Margaret what the words meant so that when she sat and listened to them rehearsing she could enjoy it even more.

Then the great day came. All the tickets were sold, except for one at the back of the hall which Clare's dad bought for Margaret.

'I'm nervous,' said Clare.

'Don't worry,' said Margaret. 'I'll be there at the back watching you. You'll be great!'

They had one last practice in the afternoon, but something dreadful happened. Clare had a sore throat and couldn't sing! Everyone was stunned. Mum and Dad couldn't believe it!

'Now we won't be able to take part at all!' said Dad. 'After all the work we've put in.'

Margaret, who had been told to keep quiet, said softly: 'I could try and sing it if you like, even though I'm not as good as Clare.'

Clare's dad said: 'Oh, you couldn't. You don't know the song or understand the words.'

'I do know the song, because I've been listening every day,' said Margaret. 'And I know what the words mean because Clare told me.'

So that night Margaret sang the song, with Larry, Phillip and Agnes. People said they'd never heard such a lovely voice before. The family won a gold cup and the audience all stood up and applauded for more than two minutes – but the loudest clapping of all came from Clare, sitting at the back of the hall.

THE POINT

We all have gifts and good things we can do. One day someone might need your gifts.

READING

But many who now are first will be last, and many who now are last will be first. *Matthew 19:30*

PRAYER

Father God,
Thank you for all the gifts you give us. Help us to use them to praise you.
Amen.

The Train Robbers

Julian, Bridie, Cyril and Heather got off the ferry at Galtarez with their mum and dad and boarded the train for Altzara. It was going to be a long journey through the night. They had paid for their two weeks holiday – the tickets and bed and breakfast in a hotel in Altzara – on the internet.

They had been warned in the brochure to be careful on the train about thieves and pickpockets, so Dad put the cases on the racks but kept his plastic bag close by his feet.

Four nice young men joined them in their compartment and soon they were all talking together. Every now and then they glanced down at Dad's plastic bag and could tell it was full of money. It was possible to see some notes at the top, and some notes were even showing from Dad's top pocket.

Mum wanted to say something but she didn't want to nag. Anyway, she was sure they were safe. These were nice young men who were chatting with them and she was sure they wouldn't steal.

The family had been travelling all the previous day and they soon grew drowsy. The train travelled on through the night and they all slept soundly. In the early hours the train stopped at little stations before getting to Altzara. At each station they woke for a few moments and then went back to sleep again.

At last, at 8 a.m., the train arrived at Altzara and they awoke to notice that the young men had got off the train earlier. Not only that, but the plastic bag had gone as well.

'They must have got off the train at one of the stations when we were half asleep,' said Heather, 'and taken all our money with them!'

'What's worse for me,' said Mum, 'is that they have even taken the few notes from Dad's top pocket. They've left us with nothing! That's what I call wicked.'

'I bet they're in a park somewhere,' said Cyril, 'sharing out the money and laughing about us.'

In the hotel room Dad sat on the bed with his head in his hands and began to shake.

Bridie put her arms round him. 'Don't cry, Dad,' she said. 'We could still have a lovely time. We could eat a big breakfast every morning to last us the day and just take walks and go to the beach.'

Then she noticed Dad wasn't crying: he was laughing his head off! Tears of laughter!

'I don't see what's funny!' said Mum.

'*Voilà!*' Dad shouted, opening his shirt and showing them a bag strapped to his chest. 'All our money is here! We're going to have a lovely time after all!'

'Magic!' Julian shouted.

'A miracle!' said Cyril. And everyone danced around the room.

'But what about the plastic bag the thieves stole from us,' said Mum, 'and the notes they took from your pocket?'

'Oh that was just toy money I took from our Monopoly game,' said Dad. 'You don't think I'm that daft, do you?'

THE POINT

God our Father will protect us from evil, but we still need to pay attention to warnings of danger and make plans to ensure that we are safe.

READING

Beware of nasty people who look like friendly, little sheep; if you look more closely, you could find that they are really wolves. Paraphrase of *Matthew 7:15*

PRAYER

Father God,

You love and protect us. Help us to be loving and caring. *Amen.*

The Truants

Tanya, Greg, Molly and Conrad liked going to Springfield School, except on Thursdays. That was school choir practice day when Miss Davis made them sing rather boring hymns for a whole hour after lunch.

At assembly on Wednesday Miss Davis said: 'Tomorrow we're having a whole day of singing. I can't tell you why yet. It's a secret but I promise you, it will make you and hundreds of other children happy.'

On Thursday Greg said: 'Let's skip school today. I bet Miss Davis just wants us to sing for her sister's playgroup, as we did last year.' And so they didn't turn up for school.

They took their lunch boxes to the park. Conrad took his CD player and they all listened to Nana Nada and the Starlights, who had just made it to number one in the charts. Molly danced to the music and Tania pretended to be in the backing group. They had a lovely time. It was much better than rehearsing nursery songs for a playgroup.

At Friday assembly Greg suddenly realised that they could be in trouble. Miss Davis might ask them where they had been. But thankfully she didn't say anything.

She didn't even notice them! She just said: 'Thank you, school, for all the hard work you put in yesterday. Nana and the Starlights were delighted. It was just what they wanted – a children's choir to back their new album for Children In Need. All the money we make will go to feed poor children. Now you have learnt all the songs, we shall be recording at their studios on Monday.'

A great cheer went out through the hall – fancy doing a record with Nana and the Starlights!

Afterwards Greg went to see Miss Davis. 'Can we come too?' he said. 'We're really good singers!'

'But you don't know the songs!' she said. 'So, I'm sorry – no – you can't be part of it.'

THE POINT

Truanting is wrong and stops us from learning. We have all been given gifts and it is good to use them to help people in need.

READING

Be on watch, be alert, for you do not know when the time will come. *Mark 13:33*

PRAYER

Father God,

Thank you for our gifts. Help us always to think of others who need our help and care. *Amen.*

The Wrong Hat

The Richmond family received an invitation to Mark and Paula's wedding. Betty, Nicholas, Garry and Georgina were very excited – they all had new clothes and there was going to be a party after the church service at the Green Fields Hotel.

'Where is this Green Fields Hotel?' Dad asked Simon. 'We don't know the town and don't want to arrive late.'

'Don't worry about that,' said Simon. 'It's only a walking distance from the church. Just follow me after the wedding.'

After the wedding they saw all the guests moving up South Street but they waited for Simon to show them the way. They waited and waited, long after all the other guests had left.

Then Mum said: 'There he is! Let's go and catch up with him.'

That was easy. It was a very hot day and you couldn't mistake the green, floppy hat Simon always wore in the summer.

Following him wasn't so easy. Garry had to do up his laces. Georgina wanted a drink of water. It all took time.

'Hurry up,' said Dad. 'Simon is walking very fast and we might lose sight of him and get lost.' They all rushed after Simon.

Mum said: 'Look at him with his floppy, green hat. You'd think he'd stop and wait for us.'

But by now he was quite a long way ahead.

They followed him from a distance. They couldn't catch up with him as he was walking too fast, even though Dad carried Betty on his shoulders and Mum carried Nicholas.

They followed him up North Street, even though the others had gone in the opposite direction.

'Don't worry,' said Dad. 'Simon knows his way around. He must be taking a short cut.'

Even so, they thought it a bit strange as they followed him from street to street. After all, he had told them the hotel was only five minutes' walk from the church.

Half an hour later – thank goodness – he stopped for a rest at the bus shelter and they were able to catch up with him.

'Simon!' Dad said. 'We've been following you. Where do we go from here for the wedding party?'

'What do you mean, wedding party?' the man said, as he took off his floppy green hat. 'I'm not called Simon! I'm Reginald Whinstone from Bradfield. You're mistaken – you've been following the wrong man.'

'Now we're lost,' Betty cried. 'And we don't even know where the wedding party is.'

'That's not my problem,' said the grumpy man.

Then suddenly Simon drove past and saw them.

'I've been driving around for the past half hour looking for you!' he shouted. 'Everyone's been waiting for you! Why didn't you follow me?'

'Because we followed the wrong man,' said Betty.

THE POINT

It is very easy to think that you are following the right person, fashion or craze. God loves us and sent Jesus into the world to show the right way to lead out lives.

READING

... he said to him, 'There is still one more thing you need to do. Sell all you have and give the money to the poor, and you will have riches in heaven; then come and follow me.' *Luke 18:22*

PRAYER

Father God,

Jesus has shown us the right way to live our lives. Help us to follow you always. *Amen.*

Thunderstorm in Woodside Park

Stockdale Town Council decided to build a bus stop and shelter at Woodside Park, because so many people went there for picnics on sunny weekends. Councillor Nichols suggested that they should get an artist to paint a picture of the park and place it in the shelter for everyone to see and admire while they were waiting for the bus.

Mayor Collins had a better idea. 'Let's have a painting competition in all our schools,' he said, 'and get a team from City College of Art to judge which one is best and we can put that one in the shelter.'

And so they did. In Mountview School Mr Fanshawe told the children about the competition. Mary painted a lovely picture of the flowers in the park. Harry painted the lawns. Hannah painted the pond. In fact, everyone painted a lovely picture – except Tim Dowling. Tim was no good at painting, but Mr Fanshawe told him to give it a try. He decided to do as he was told, and planned to call his painting 'Sunshine in Woodside Park'.

He painted the sun, the flowers and the pond but it looked awful. Bully Barnwell, who sat next to him, kept nudging his elbow as he was painting, which made the picture even worse. The yellows ran into the reds, the reds into the blues, the blues ran into the pinks. Then Bully Barnwell poured black paint over the top corner – just for a laugh, you know! By now, the picture really was a mess. Tim tried to brush down the black but it only ran into the blue and made the picture worse.

At three o'clock Mr Fanshawe collected the pictures and everyone laughed when they saw Tim's. 'What's this supposed to be?' said Mr Fanshawe.

'Sunshine in Woodside Park!' said Tim.

Bully Barnwell sneered and said: 'Looks more like a messy thunderstorm to me.'

'Then that's what we'll call it,' said Mr Fanshawe. 'Don't be ashamed, Tim: you did your best.'

Three days later Sir Richard Lattimer, Lady Winslow and Lady Carder from the College of Art came to judge the pictures and were not all that impressed by most of them – until they came to Tim's.

'By Jolly Jove!' Sir Richard called to the other judges. 'Come and look at this! Thunderstorm in Woodside Park! It's amazing! Look at the colours – the way they splash into each other: the pinks, the blues, the reds and those bold black strokes coming down from the clouds above!'

Lady Winslow and Lady Carder agreed. They had never seen work so different, special or outstanding, apart from modern galleries in Paris and Berlin.

Of course, Tim never painted another picture. He wouldn't dare. But now, when he drives the 72B from Town Square and stops at Woodside Park, he can't help laughing to himself. There are still people coming to see the outstanding picture of a Thunderstorm in Woodside Park.

THE POINT

God works through each one of us in wonderful ways.

READING

To him who by means of his power working in us is able to do so much more than we can ever ask for, or even think of ... *Ephesians 3: 20*

PRAYER

Father God,

You are wonderful. May all we do bring us closer to you and make other people happy. *Amen.*

Together Again

The Whitmore family decided they would all go on a self-catering holiday together at Sorbian, where they had booked a farmhouse. 'Sheer bliss!' thought Mum and Dad. 'No phones, no TV, no computers and no newspapers for two weeks. Just time together.'

They filled the car with all they needed. It was a big car with plenty of space for Ron, Katy, Sam and Polly.

There was no room for Gran and Grandad, so they travelled the day before by plane. That was a good idea because they were rather old and frail and the journey by car would have been too much for them.

'See you in Sorbian tomorrow,' they all said.

On the first day in Sorbian, Gran and Grandad went to the market and bought loads of food. They wanted to have a lovely dinner ready for the family when they arrived.

The Whitmores got as far as Rabiana when the car broke down. The garages were closed so they had to book into a hotel for the night. They couldn't phone Gran at the farmhouse because there wasn't a phone there!

The next day the man at the garage said they'd need a spare part which might take another few days to come, so they had to stay in Rabiana for three more days.

All this time Gran and Grandad were waiting in Sorbian for the family to arrive, wondering why they hadn't come.

At last the Whitmores got away, but when they came to Orofino they were told they could go no further because of repairs to the bridge. They would have to go north to Urbana and cut across to Marinas. That was a very, very long way round!

At Marinas, Ron felt sick. It might be nothing – maybe just the heat – but Mum wouldn't take chances. They went to the hospital, and the doctors said Ron should spend the night in hospital, just in case.

Meanwhile, in Sorbian, Gran and Grandad were still wondering why they hadn't arrived.

In Marinas, next day, the doctor said Ron would be all right and so they set off again. By the time they got to Alvarez, Dad was exhausted. The children were tired and Mum thought this was no holiday at all. So they stayed there for two days. It was safer than driving on and turned out to be a nice little break.

At Tirana the town was closed from traffic for two days for the Festival of Saint Gerardo. There was no way through, but the family was told they could go back north to Hirondo and take the coastal road from there. That was a very long way to go! But they did it!

At Hirondo the car broke down again. The man at the garage said: 'Whoever mended your car the last time didn't know what they were doing. No wonder you've broken down again! But I can get it fixed properly in a day or two.'

From Hirondo they drove to Frascano and stayed there for a night – because it was better for Dad than to continue driving when he was tired!

At last they arrived at Sorbian, but it was the last day of their holiday. What a waste! But they all had a lovely meal together.

'Why did it take you so long?' said Gran. 'We were waiting for you.'

'It doesn't matter now,' said Polly. 'We're all together again – just like we'll be in heaven.'

THE POINT

We all want to be together in heaven one day, with all our friends and those we love, but sometimes it takes a long time.

READING

We, however, are citizens of heaven, and we eagerly wait for our Saviour, the Lord Jesus Christ, to come from heaven. *Philippians 3:20*

PRAYER

Father God,

Thank you for our families. Help us to be loving and caring children. *Amen.*

Uncle Arthur's Surprise

Lora, Ben, Sam and Wendy were mad about trains, so Mum and Dad said they would give them a special present at Christmas. And so they did. They saved up plenty of money and on Christmas Day they gave them a present for all of them to share. It was a model railway track and a train for each one of them. Lora called hers Dart Express; Ben's was named Superspeed; Sam went for Railstar; Wendy's was Wonder-rail.

All week they played with their trains, taking it in turns to use the track.

Then Dad said: 'Next Sunday we're going to see my Uncle Arthur. He lives all alone and would be so happy to see us all.'

Mum said: 'We should take him a present, but we've spent all our money over Christmas. What can we give him? I know. What about that coffee maker you gave me last year? We've never used it and Uncle Arthur would be delighted to have one. It would make him very happy.'

Dad said: 'Excellent idea.' And they wrapped it up in a yellow box with red ribbons and a card which said: 'We love you, Uncle Arthur.'

Sam said: 'We can show him our present.'

And so they took their trains to show to Uncle Arthur.

Uncle Arthur was delighted to see them. Wendy put down the train set on the carpet. Dad brought out the yellow box. 'We've got something special to give you,' he said.

Uncle Arthur was overjoyed. They'd never seen him so happy. 'You are too kind,' he said. 'How can I thank you? This is what I've always wanted, ever since I was a little boy!'

And with that, he picked up the train set.

'But…' said Wendy.

'Shussh,' Dad whispered. 'We've made an old man very happy.'

THE POINT

Sometimes, giving to others and making them happy is better than getting things for ourselves.

READING

The King will reply, 'I tell you, whenever you did this for one of the least important of these members of my family, you did it for me. *Matthew 25:40*

PRAYER

Father God,

Help us to care for and love the poor and the lonely. *Amen.*

Uncle Charlie's Cherry Choir

Uncle Charlie used to be famous. He conducted choirs in many cathedrals in the land. Some of the performances were even broadcast on TV. But those days are over and he spends most of his time sitting outside the back door of his cottage looking at the cherry trees in his garden.

Frank, Wendy, Sally and Harry used to visit him on their way home from school and bring him biscuits, as he couldn't get out any more – not even on Sundays to go to church.

'I don't mind,' he told them. 'I can pray in the garden and every year, when my cherries ripen, a beautiful choir comes down from the skies. They sing God's praises and I conduct them. Then we all have a feast of cherries together. Perhaps, one day, you can come and join us, but you had better come early – they only come at the break of dawn and don't stay very long.'

Dad said that Uncle Charlie really did think that choirs from the sky came down to sing with him in the morning but that could never happen.

Mum said: 'Let the children stay with your brother for a night and then they will see for themselves in the morning.'

So Wendy, Sally, Harry and Frank went to stay the night. The children couldn't get to sleep that night in Uncle Charlie's cottage. Wendy thought that his choir might be angels, but Sally said they could be fairies.

Just before dawn Uncle Charlie called them. 'They're coming!' he shouted.

The children ran out and waited as the sun rose. All was silent. Nothing happened!

'Dad was right,' thought Harry. 'Uncle Charlie was just pretending.'

Then, from the skies, twenty blackbirds flew down on to the cherry tree, pecking the cherries and chirping their songs. Uncle Charlie stood up and waved his arms, just like he did when he conducted the cathedral choirs.

'Now, this is my choir,' he said, 'for every creature gives glory and praise to God.'

THE POINT

Everything we see and hear was made by God and gives him praise.

READING

In the trees near by, the birds make their nests and sing. *Psalm 104:12*

PRAYER

Father God,

Thank you for all you have made. Let us sing your praise for ever. *Amen.*

Uncle Harry's Car

Uncle Harry was very proud of his Riana Rowlett car and he kept it in perfect condition, even though it was nearly as old as him! Every Sunday he took Clara, Jason, Mandy and Bert for a ride in it. Then one Sunday it broke down. The clutch had gone. Even so, Uncle Harry wasn't troubled. 'It's just worn out,' he said. 'I'll call the garage.'

So they got out of the car and waited on the grass verge for the breakdown recovery.

The man from the garage said he would put in a new clutch and that Uncle Harry could pick it up on Thursday. Uncle Harry said he had to see the doctor on Thursday about his bad elbow but could pick it up on Friday, which he did.

The following Sunday it was so wet and dark that even in the afternoon Uncle Harry had to put on the headlights – but they didn't work.

'We'd better call the garage again,' he said. So the children stepped out of the car and huddled under an umbrella while they waited for the breakdown recovery man to come.

'The battery's run out,' said the man from the garage. 'I'll get a new one on Monday.'

But Uncle Harry told him that on Monday he had to see the optician about his new glasses. He could pick up the car on Tuesday.

The following Sunday the exhaust fell off. The followed the same routine – stepped out of the car and waited for the man from garage. When he got there he said he'd have it ready by Tuesday – but Uncle Harry had an appointment with the dentist for his new teeth so said he would pick it up on Wednesday.

The following Sunday it was the ignition! The car wouldn't start after they'd stopped for a picnic. So once again, they stepped out of the car and waited for the man from the garage.

When he arrived he said: 'Harry, you're wasting your time and money. That old car is worn out. It's had its day. You'd be better off getting rid of it.'

Uncle Harry agreed, but was sad to see the car that had served him so well for so many, many years, taken away. So were the children.

'Never mind,' said Uncle Harry. 'I'll get a new one! Then we'll have lots of rides in my new one, for years and years to come.'

Two weeks later Uncle Harry died, and the children were in tears at his funeral.

Dad said: 'Don't cry. Uncle Harry hasn't gone for ever. He's just stepped out of his car and is waiting for us to arrive later.'

THE POINT
Death comes to all. God's promise is of eternal life with him for ever.

READING
God will wipe away all tears from our eyes; there will be no more death, and no more mourning or sadness. *Paraphrase of Revelation 21:4*

PRAYER
Father God,
We are very sad when someone we love dies. Help us to know that they are happy with you and waiting to welcome us. *Amen.*